ROAD TRIPS
THROUGH HISTORY

A COLLECTION OF ESSAYS FROM PRESERVATION MAGAZINE

BY DWIGHT YOUNG

INTRODUCTION

BY RICHARD MOE
President of the National Trust

A quirky bit of roadside architecture (the restaurant shaped like a coffee pot or doughnut) can bring forth a chuckle; the soaring columns and sparkling stained glass in an urban cathedral can inspire awe and wonder; the familiar corridors and banks of windows in older school buildings can touch off memories of favorite teachers and childhood best friends; and the long rows of grave markers in a Civil War battlefield can bring a quiet sadness as you reflect on the many young lives lost during that turbulent time.

Historic architecture and places bring out many emotions. Compelling and thoughtful writing can elicit the same responses — a laugh out loud, a nod of agreement, or a poignant recollection of a sad event. Over the years, Dwight Young's essays have been doing just that — making us smile, reflect, and look at the world around us with a fresh eye.

Fifty-four of Dwight's columns, which have appeared since 1992 on the "Back Page" in each issue of *Preservation* magazine, have been reprinted here — from his first column in June 1992 on the importance of preserving battlefields to his July/August 2003 essay on front porches. You can continue to catch the new ones every other month in your copy of *Preservation* magazine. Dwight's official title at the National Trust is Senior Communications Associate, and in his 26 years here he has done everything from running our historic sites to our regional offices. But most importantly, he has become the institutional memory of the entire preservation movement — as well as the National Trust's most eloquent voice.

Since its inception, the "Back Page" — humorous, thought-provoking, heartwarming, and inspiring — has been one of the most popular features of our magazine. I know for a fact that many of our magazine readers skip to the back of *Preservation* to read Dwight's essay before they look at anything else. He writes about famous and not-so-famous preservationists, well-known and little-known historic places, and about his adventures — often as the National Trust representative on our Study Tours program — traveling to small towns and exotic faraway lands.

In his essay "The Great Preservation Novel" Dwight laments the fact that no one has written the great preservation novel — the story of a true preservation triumph, complete with sneaky officials and greedy landowners trying to destroy a revered historic site and noble heroes to save the day. But perhaps we don't need a preservation *War and Peace*. Maybe we need to keep a copy of *Road Trips through History* handy for a reassuring and thoughtful perspective on historic places and the stories they tell.

TABLE OF CONTENTS

DOWNTOWN: HANDLE WITH CARE

Sometime in the 1960s, sinister forces put something in the national water supply that made us temporarily nuts. That's the only way to explain the awful things that have been done to too many American downtowns in the past few decades.

Look at what happened to Rockville, Md., for example. Just over 20 years ago, Rockville went in for urban renewal in a big way. A sizeable chunk of downtown was razed, and in its place rose the Rockville Mall. Articles in the local papers have often said unkind things about the mall, describing it variously as "a disaster," a "hulking concrete eyesore," and "a largely vacant monolith plagued by poor design and bad luck since its opening." With reviews like those, it's no wonder the mall's owners have announced that they'd like to knock the thing down.

This is the part that intrigues me: They want to replace it with something "more closely resembling a city center of yesteryear" — which, as far as I can tell, is what they tore down around 1970. The new development will be "designed to look and feel pretty much like the bustling village Rockville once was," with streets that will be "accessible to pedestrians and cars." In other words, it's a total switcheroo: Out with

the old newfangled downtown, in with the new old-fashioned downtown.

Well, I hope it works, but the whole thing strikes me as a sad example of Americans' seeming inability to avoid the temptation to mess around with their business districts. These efforts to "fix" downtown can range from merely misguided to downright stupid.

Consider, as an example of low-key muddle-headedness, the new lights that were installed on Main Street in Columbia, S.C., some years ago. These were no ordinary lights; they were huge megawatt football-stadium lights on tall metal poles. Planted in the middle of the street like a row of steel sequoias, these towers managed to obliterate the view of the state capitol dome that had always been downtown's major focal point. Fortunately, the lights didn't last very long (astronauts in outer space probably complained about the glare) and the view of the statehouse was eventually restored — though not, one assumes, without considerable expense.

Much more extreme is the case of Helen, a small town in the North Georgia mountains that transformed itself into a Bavarian village — complete with Hansel-and-Gretel architecture, signs in Gothic script, and a half-timbered Olde Towne clock tower that could house a cuckoo the size of a pterodactyl. When I saw the place, it seemed that everything stationary had a basket of geraniums hanging from it, and everything ambulatory was wearing a dirndl or lederhosen. Heidis yodeled. Glockenspiels tinkled. I got out of there fast.

Sometimes it takes a sales pitch for a new commercial development to open our eyes to the quirky things that make a traditional downtown unique. The reborn Rockville, for instance, will include streets for cars and pedestrians. *What a concept!*

Recent Christmas advertisements for another new downtown in the Washington suburbs, the Reston Town Center, urged shoppers to forsake enclosed malls for the thrill of walking from store to store on an actual sidewalk exposed to the actual open air. *Outdoors! What will they think of next?*

Downtowns are fragile things, easily injured. They should have "Handle with Care" stickers plastered all over them. Lots of them need help, but they

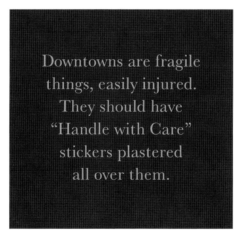

Downtowns are fragile things, easily injured. They should have "Handle with Care" stickers plastered all over them.

don't need to be turned into something else altogether. While such groups as the National Trust's National Main Street Center have had great success in conveying that message, too many people — public officials, planners, merchants, shoppers — still don't get it.

So here's my plan: We'll go to Bavaria, see, and find a pretty little village tucked away somewhere. Then we'll convince the townspeople to transform their village into a lock-stock-and-barrel replica of a typical American downtown: a courthouse square with a Civil War monument on one corner, a five-and-dime, a drugstore, a barber shop with a dentist's office upstairs — you know, the whole works. American tourists will discover the place and be charmed by it. They'll ask one another, "How come we don't have anything like this back in the States?" And sooner or later one of them will say, "Wait a minute, we do!"

The scary thing is, it just might work.

STARRY, STARRY SIGHT

When I was a kid in Texas, sometimes on hot summer nights we'd drag a mattress outdoors and sleep in the back yard. Those at-home campouts were always both unnerving and awe-inspiring. Unnerving because we were sure that every rustle we heard — and there was an amazing amount of rustling going on in that yard — was made by roving bands of rattlesnakes or coyotes, every one of them looking for a kid to bite. Awe-inspiring because of the night sky.

Our town had no industry to speak of, and our neighborhood, as I recall, didn't even have streetlights, so there was nothing to dim the brilliance of the stars. We'd lie on our backs and pick out the Big Dipper and the Milky Way (the only two celestial landmarks we knew by name) and then, inevitably, we'd fall silent, awestruck — there really is no other word for it — by the vast, glittering spectacle overhead.

That kind of experience is hard to come by these days. When I gaze heavenward from my teensy Capitol Hill back yard, the view is decidedly uninspiring. Instead of the inky black I remember from childhood, the sky is a sort of milky blue-gray. There aren't many lights up there, and many of those that are visible turn out to be planes headed for the recently renamed Ronald Reagan Washington National Airport.

Washington isn't the only place where a dark, star-spangled sky is an increasingly — and distressingly — rare commodity. Even on the remotest rural byway, every gas station is lit up like Times Square, and every parking lot on every small-town commercial strip is awash in wattage from street-lights and searchlights and spotlights and floodlights galore. Thanks to this overabundance of illumination, you can, if you're so inclined, pause on the curb in front of the convenience store at 3 a.m. and read the fine print on a beef-jerky wrapper with no trouble at all. What you can't do is see the stars.

The technical term for this prob-lem is "light spillage" or "light tres-pass." Whatever you call it, it's robbing us of something fundamental and beautiful, and a growing number of people have decided it's time to hit the dimmer switch.

A short while back, the New Mexico legislature passed the Night Sky Protection Act, prohibiting future installation of glaring mercury-vapor fixtures and requiring that most out-door lighting be shielded so that light is directed downward, not up. Other states and communities from Maine to Arizona have enacted similar laws, but what makes the New Mexico legislation really interesting is the fact that the major push for its enactment came from the New Mexico Heritage Preservation Alliance, which put the night sky on its first annual endangered sites list three months before the legislature acted.

So preservationists have successfully taken on the challenge of saving the very heavens above. Let me just say this about that: YEAH!

Preservation is all about having the good sense to hang on to things that are meaningful and enduring — and

few things fit this description better than the starry sky that guided, awed, and inspired our forefathers, from Renaissance scientists to Native American shamans. An appreciation of the glory overhead is part of our cultural legacy from the past, and protecting it is a valid part of our mission to preserve the "spirit of place" that was the theme of this year's National Preservation Conference.

What's more, new technology and smarter installation practices enable us to put light where it's needed without compromising safety. We don't have to stumble in the darkness, but neither do we have to "illuminate the bellies of birds," as one crusader put it, with glare that turns midnight into noon.

Pick up a copy of Chet Raymo's *An Intimate Look at the Night Sky* (Walker & Company, 2001) and read what the author has to say about stargazing. Then, on a clear night, just go outside and look up. You'll see why it's important to save the dark sky — and the sense of wonder that gets lost in the light.

Music to Our Eyes

During the 2002 National Preservation Conference in Cleveland, I paid my first visit to Severance Hall, which may be the most gorgeous concert hall in the country, and the Rock and Roll Hall of Fame, which is now firmly lodged near the top of my personal Favorite Places list. Since then I've been thinking about music and buildings and preservation.

From George Gershwin to Janis Joplin, from bluegrass and the blues to rap and the Broadway show tune, popular music is America's biggest and best-known export. Millions of people in other countries don't know a thing about daily life in the United States, but they sure as heck know how America *sounds*. Maybe we didn't (to quote that old Coca-Cola commercial) "teach the world to sing," but we certainly gave the world a bright, new — and distinctively American — song.

Music is the soundtrack of our lives — and our buildings. When Goethe described architecture as frozen music, he knew exactly what he was talking about. Think "cathedral" and your head immediately fills with the thundering chords of a Bach fugue. A glass-walled skyscraper plays a Henry Mancini tune, exuding sleek sophistication from every spandrel. Art Deco sounds like jazz, and I defy anyone to drive through a ranch-house subdivision without hearing the relentlessly peppy theme from *Leave It to Beaver* or *The Brady Bunch*.

It's not surprising that music-related buildings are getting considerable attention from preservationists. Right now, the National Trust's Save America's Treasures program is helping preserve the historic Chess Records studio in Chicago. Like the Sun Records building in Memphis (where Elvis made his first recording) and Detroit's Hitsville USA complex (the original home of Motown Records), the Chess studio isn't much to look at — but who cares? Songs recorded here by artists such as Muddy Waters, Etta James, Bo Diddley, and Aretha Franklin have become part of mankind's musical language. Chess records have traveled all over the world, and beyond: The Rolling Stones immortalized the studio's address — 2120 South Michigan Avenue — in the title of a 1960s instrumental, and Chuck Berry's "Johnny B. Goode" was included on a record sent into the outer reaches of the solar system by NASA in 1977.

Given all of this, it was a pretty big shock to learn recently that one of Washington's most significant musical landmarks had bitten the dust before anyone knew what was happening.

In the 1920s, a ragtime pianist named Louis Thomas opened up a popular cabaret on the ground floor of a turn-of-the-century rowhouse at 9th and R Streets. A young Washington native named Edward Ellington — everyone called him "Duke" — frequently played piano there when he was just getting started in the music biz. As the launching-pad for Ellington's career, the building could have become a major attraction in the burgeoning Shaw neighborhood — but that won't happen now, because there's nothing left of it.

Citing its deteriorated condition, the city told the owner to fix it or flatten it, and the owner — despite Washington's tough law against demolition by neglect, and despite a flurry of last-minute efforts to call off the bulldozers — had it bashed to rubble. Preservationists and city officials engaged in the requisite hand-wringing over the unnecessary loss of a landmark, but the fuss, like the dust at 9th and R, eventually settled down. The owner plans to build condos on the site, probably adorned with one of those "On This Site Formerly Stood…" signs.

In the 1970s, Simon and Garfunkel recorded a wistful little love song called "So Long, Frank Lloyd Wright." It has a delicately pretty tune and adoring lyrics:

Architects may come
and architects
may go,
And never change
your point of view.
When I run dry,
I stop awhile and
think of you.

Oddly enough, it's the only song about an architect that I know of. No one, it seems, has gotten around to writing "Moonlight and Roses and Henry Hobson Richardson" or "Hey Hey, I. M. Pei."

No matter. While there may not be much music about buildings, there are lots of buildings about music — but not so many that we can afford to let the wrecking-ball silence the melody.

Lost at Sea

The Ocean Liner Museum, a collection without a permanent home port, has temporarily dropped anchor at Manhattan's PaineWebber Gallery and is mounting an exhibition that ranges from steamer trunks to postcards and a steward's jacket from the *George Washington*. My palms are sweaty with anticipation.

I collect this stuff, you see. It's a passion for which there doesn't seem to be a name. Stamp collectors are philatelists and wine lovers are oenophiles, but my only label is the pedestrian "collector of ocean-liner memorabilia." It's a hobby that occupies a lot of my spare time and a lot of space in my house.

While I'm proud of the ship models, ashtrays, souvenirs, china, and flatware that line my shelves, it's the paper items that intrigue me most. Show me a pile of paper at a flea market and I'll paw through it for hours, looking for ocean-liner menus or brochures or baggage labels — and finding them with surprising and gratifying frequency.

This ephemera (a much nicer term than "paper stuff") can be appreciated on many levels. Much of it is beautifully designed: Menus from Belgium's Red Star Line of the 1920s, for example, are Art Deco gems. Italian Line advertisements from the 1930s entice the eye with beguiling drawings of fashion-plate passengers in languid poses on theatrically overscaled staircases and around gargantuan swimming pools.

Equally fascinating are the pieces that exhibit the original owner's personality: I prize a passenger list on which a certain Miss Newman of Cincinnati, steaming through the Caribbean on the *Haiti* in 1934, wrote wickedly catty descriptions of her shipmates.

But the best thing about this mass of colorful paper is the fact that it links me with an immensely appealing slice of the vanished past. Perhaps it's no accident that the words "collection" and "connection" are so similar. Handling fragile pages, I am connected to a time when these majestic vessels were symbols of national pride and paradigms of glamour. I become part of an era when Cunard's *Aquitania* was "The Ship Beautiful," her lavish interiors meant to suggest "a stately home of England put to sea"; when the *United States*, arguably the best-looking liner ever built, looked racy even while standing still; when the unmatched mystique of France's *Normandie* ("O ship of light…") made her the epitome of sleek sophistication.

Too many of these gorgeous behemoths came to a sad end. The *Normandie* capsized at her New York pier in 1942 while being converted to wartime use. The *Queen Elizabeth*, her glory days long past, burned in Hong Kong harbor in 1972. The *Ile de France* suffered the unkindest fate of all: She was battered, blasted, and humiliated in the making of a thoroughly forgettable 1960 movie called *The Last Voyage*.

A handful remains. The *Queen Mary* is now a hotel, looking lovely but somewhat ill at ease in the midst of California sunshine and palm trees. Sister ships *Independence* and *Constitution* (*I Love Lucy* fans will recall that the *Constitution* ferried Lucy and company to Europe in 1956) cruise Hawaiian waters. While the long-neglected *United States* awaits a renovation than never seems to happen, the dowager *Monterey*, which entered service in 1932, sails on as the *Britanis*.

I'm going to New York for the exhibition, of course. Maybe I'll go down to the tip of Manhattan, where the Cunard Building still stands at 25 Broadway and the nearby Custom House has wonderful ocean-liner murals in its rotunda. I may even trek over to Brooklyn Heights to see the two sets of doors from the *Normandie* that now grace the Church of Our Lady of Lebanon.

When I get home I'll sift through my collection, marveling at how this flimsy passenger list (*Carmania*, February 1906) managed to survive all these years, and wondering whether the brownish stain on this menu (*Paris*, 13 May 1929) was left by a drop of wine or *sauce bearnaise*. And I'll fret because my own past doesn't stretch back far enough to encompass the heyday of these ghost ships.

E. B. White once wrote, "I heard the *Queen Mary* blow one midnight…and the sound carried the whole history of departure and longing and loss." If you ask me, the only thing sadder than that sound is the absence of it.

UPDATE: After years in storage, the extensive collections of the Ocean Liner Museum were transferred in 2002 to New York's South Street Seaport, which already displays numerous ocean-liner items in its Walter Lord Gallery. Additional information is available at www.southstseaport.org.

The lost-liner list continues to grow. The 68-year-old *Monterey* sank off South Africa in 2000 while being towed to the scrap yard. The *Constitution* met the same fate in the Pacific in 1997. But there is some good news. In May 2003, Norwegian Cruise Lines announced that it had bought the glorious *United States*, which had languished in rusty solitude for more than three decades, and the *Independence*, which had been retired in 2001. NCL says that the two ships, once the pride of the American passenger fleet, will be rebuilt and returned to active service.

THE ESSENCE OF EXCELLENCE

Communities can win acclaim for any number of things. For example, I am prepared to state unequivocally (having done extensive research into the subject) that Santa Fe in winter smells better than any other American city, and New Orleans in spring has the most interesting litter.

Scattered portions of other cities smell good, too. In San Francisco there's a spot on Polk Street where, in addition to the mix of salt air and eucalyptus that permeates the whole area, you get a sudden whiff of baking bread that is bound to send you rushing into the nearest doughnut shop for something yeasty, preferably with a sugar glaze. And in Natchez, Miss., I took a walk one summer evening through a neighborhood where the smell of honeysuckle, gardenias, and magnolias was so strong that I staggered back to my hotel in a state of olfactory overload. Even part of downtown Baltimore used to smell good when the spice factory was in operation — but the factory didn't survive the revitalization of the Inner Harbor, and now the area reeks of designer labels and street-mime makeup.

Aroma-wise, Santa Fe is in a league of its own, especially on starry winter nights. The air is perfumed — there's no other word for it — with cedar and pine and the faint but unmistakable scent of snow, plus an occasional hint of something delectable cooking. And there's something else — I think it's the piñon wood burning in hundreds of fireplaces — that makes the place smell like a giant incense burner. You smile with every breath; you want to pin a medal on the whole town.

Sidewalk litter usually doesn't inspire the medal-pinning impulse. Understandably so, since cracks in the sidewalks of most cities tend to collect nothing more interesting than cigarette butts and, at certain times of the year, dead leaves and patches of gray ice. But New Orleans is different. In the spring, cracks in the French Quarter sidewalks are likely to fill up with stray plastic beads and miniature drifts of glitter.

Even outside the Quarter an observant stroller may spot some interesting stuff underfoot. Walking down Magazine Street a few months ago, I couldn't help wondering why the gutters were full of cabbage leaves. (An explosion in a nearby sauerkraut factory? A salad bar for stray dogs?) Eventually an obliging storekeeper informed me that the cabbage leaves were left over from a recent St. Patrick's Day parade. This was not surprising, since New Orleanians have a parade for every occasion, most of them involving floats from which riders throw trinkets or candy — or, in this case, vegetables.

Admittedly, ordinary litter is not something to be encouraged, but a city block paved with cabbage leaves or spangled with purple sequins is not exactly ordinary. That's why I have no doubt that if the new Great American Main Street Awards honored intriguing trash, first prize would go to New Orleans. And if the awards were passed out in recognition of overall aromatic excellence, Santa Fe would win hands down.

But that's not what the Great American Main Street Awards are about. Presented for the first time this year, these awards are not about smells, but about sounds. The sound of coins dropping into a cash register, the sound of an awning being rolled out to shade crowds of shoppers, the sound of hammers and saws as storefronts are renovated, the sounds of voices and footsteps as people move in and out of shops and offices. The healthy sound of a community's heartbeat.

And the awards are not about trash, but about treasure. The treasure of buildings and people and traditions that lies at the core of every town. A treasure celebrated in nostalgic books and movies but often overlooked or abandoned in real life. A treasure rediscovered, burnished to a high gloss and put to vibrant use by the five communities — Clarksville, Mo.; Dubuque, Iowa; Franklin, Tenn.; Pasadena, Calif.; and Sheboygan Falls, Wisc. — that won this year's awards.

The National Main Street Center marks its 15th anniversary this year. That's good cause for celebration (if we were in New Orleans, there'd be a parade), with the winning communities as the brightest candles on the birthday cake. They may not have glitter-strewn sidewalks, but these Main Streets have extraordinary spirit. They may not smell like incense, but they smell like something even better: success.

DREAM HOUSE

As a participant in the Experiment in International Living, I spent the summer of 1964 in Nigeria. In the city of Zaria I lived for a few days in a mansion made of mud. At its center was a noisy courtyard where things went on: clothes-washing and chicken-plucking, adults' arguments and children's games. Leading from this courtyard to my room was a long, dark hallway that sometimes had a goat in it. My room sported fussy Victorian furniture, crocheted doilies, and a luridly tinted photo of Queen Elizabeth in her coronation robes — all topped off with a thatched ceiling where unseen creatures rustled ominously in the night. It was, all in all, the most marvelous place I've ever lived in.

I thought about that house recently while leafing through a magazine called *Robb Report* (subtitle: *"for the luxury lifestyle"*). Tucked among the ads for home theater seating, extravagantly complicated wristwatches and a watch-winding gizmo to provide "Long Term Health Care" for them, and a humdinger of a mattress ("two miles of vanadium-treated premiere grade wire" swaddled in "the purest Asian cashmere, soft New Zealand lambs wool and rich cotton felt from the American Deep South") was a photo spread in which parts of 11 different houses had been cobbled together to create "The Ultimate Home."

Ultimate, maybe. Eye-popping, definitely.

The facade, a cool assemblage of glass and white aluminum panels, came from a Dallas house designed by Richard Meier. Inside, the foyer was a 40-foot-high Beaux-Arts rotunda with a spiral staircase and plasterwork seemingly carved out of buttercream frosting. The bedroom was a minimalist breath of space with glass walls and angular furniture that appeared to float above the bare floors. As for the bathroom — well, if you're the type who likes to loll in a pool of asses' milk strewn with rose petals, this green marble grotto looked like the perfect place to do it in.

I immediately set to work assembling my own Ultimate Home, using rooms from historic buildings. It was a challenge.

First impressions are terribly important — so for the entry hall, I chose the Great Hall at the Library of Congress, a multi-columned, murals-and-marble extravaganza that knocks me out every time I see it. It's a gasp-inducing space, and gasps are exactly what you want to hear when guests step into your Ultimate Entry Hall.

For the living room, I picked the hall at Craigievar Castle in Scotland.

Even though it's in a no-kidding 17th-century castle, it's a fairly intimate room, with an ornate vaulted ceiling, racks of antlers on the walls, and fat sofas covered in plaid. Very cozy and country-housey. Very, very Ultimate.

Years ago I spent a night in a real southern plantation house. I slept in a room that had a covey of angels carved in the fireplace mantel, a huge mahogany four-poster bed, and floor-to-ceiling windows opening onto a sunny verandah overlooking a field where cows and chickens were displayed in picturesquely bucolic poses. That's the bedroom I chose, complete with angels and livestock.

For the bathroom, I thought briefly about Drayton Hall, where an intriguing 19th-century drawing shows a seven-hole privy fitted out with comfy-looking chairbacks. Fortunately I came to my senses and decided to go with the glitzy bathroom in *Robb Report*. I know it's not from an old house — but in a bathroom you don't need history, you need three acres of green marble.

That's it, except for a few odds and ends. Like the view from Olana, Frederick Church's aerie overlooking the Hudson River, and the front door of Greene & Greene's Gamble House in Pasadena. I'll fit them in somewhere.

Choosing a facade was difficult (Philip Johnson's Glass House? South Dakota's Corn Palace?), but finally I realized that nothing would do but that mud mansion in Zaria. Admittedly, there's a pretty serious disconnect between the understated earthen exterior and the sumptuous interiors I've assembled — but when you're building The Ultimate Home, you can't be bound by the niggling minutiae of spatial reality.

What *really* worries me is how long it's going to take to fill that enormous bathtub. Somebody better start milking those asses right now.

BATTLEFIELDS

Recently, more than a century and a quarter after the Civil War clash that made it famous, the Brandy Station battlefield has been in the news again.

The Virginia legislature has enacted a measure that may result in the battlefield's being "delisted" from the Virginia Landmarks Register. In other words, the legislature in its wisdom (or, in response to pressure from developers) has decreed that the site of the largest cavalry engagement ever fought in North America may not be historic after all. At least not *officially* historic.

The whole thing has the ring of familiarity to most preservationists, who recall the struggle to save a portion of the Manassas battlefield from inappropriate development a few years ago.

Why all the fuss over battlefields? They are, after all, just parts of the landscape, often with little remaining above ground to remind a casual visitor of what happened there. In fact, one Virginia solon, attempting to downplay Brandy Station's significance, said that it was "just a big open field." (What, I wonder, does he expect a battlefield to look like?)

In attempting to understand why we place so much importance on these "big open fields," the following quote from Czech President Vaclav Havel may be instructive:

We still don't know how to put morality ahead of politics, science, and economics. We are still incapable of understanding that the only genuine backbone of all our actions, if they are to be moral, is responsibility. Responsibility to something higher than my family, my country, my success — responsibility to the order of being where all our actions are indelibly recorded and where and only where they will be properly judged....

Perhaps if all national leaders were playwrights — or, at the very least, if all national leaders spoke and thought that way — we wouldn't have wars, and we wouldn't have battlefields. But they aren't, and we do.

Battlefields are important to us because they are signposts, marking the way we've come in our long, slow progress up from the dark — and also, sadly, marking the times and places where we slipped backward into the dark again for a while. For every battlefield by its very nature is evidence of failure on someone's part: failure to find peaceful solutions, failure to accept the "responsibility to something higher" that Havel talks about, failure to keep us — all of us as human beings — away from the terrifying morass of mud and blood that always waits to engulf us.

A battlefield confronts us with our own transgressions. It admonishes us to learn from past mistakes or, in a phrase no less pithy for being somewhat hackneyed, be doomed to repeat them. We need battlefields for that reason: We need to remember, to be warned.

But they're important for another reason, too, and it is reflected in another passage from Vaclav Havel:

> When Thomas Jefferson wrote that "governments are instituted among men, deriving their just powers from the consent of the governed," it was a simple and important act of the human spirit. What gave meaning to that act, however, was the fact that the author backed it up with his life. It was not just his words; it was his deeds as well.

We care so much for our battlefields because they are arenas in which words became deeds, brave or foolhardy or both. On a battlefield, whether Hastings or Iwo Jima or Little Bighorn, we stand on a spot where people demonstrated that they cared enough about something to stop talking about it and to turn instead to action.

It really doesn't matter much whether we feel that they acted correctly or not. We respect their commitment, may even envy the depth of feeling that drove them to take up arms. We honor their sacrifice. We mark the spots where they stood and fell. We turn their battlegrounds into places of pilgrimage.

No wonder, then, that threats to the sanctity of these battlefields generate such tremendous outpourings of emotion. We cannot afford to lose these haunted, haunting places. They are essential to our knowledge of ourselves. They are mirrors reflecting at once our worst and best faces.

UPDATE: As feared, Brandy Station battlefield was removed from the Virginia Landmarks Register "by legislative direction" in 1993.

We've all heard the old cliché that the Civil War isn't over yet in the South. It's certainly true that fighting continues to rage at battlefields all over the region. Since 1988, the National Trust's annual list of America's 11 Most Endangered Historic Places has included five Civil War battlefields in Virginia alone — plus others in Maryland, Mississippi, and Pennsylvania.

There have been some important preservation victories in 2003 — in January Congress created a new national park to protect the Cedar Creek battlefield in the Shenandoah Valley, and in March a developer failed to gain approval for his proposed new community on a portion of the Chancellorsville battlefield — but no one believes the last shot has been fired.

NOPE TO TAUPE

Across the street from my office window, right in the middle of a historic district, some guys recently painted a turn-of-the-century rowhouse blue. Not some pantywaist robins-egg tint. We're talking **BLUE** here, the color of those berry-flavored snow cones that turn your tongue a most gruesome shade. Put a thousand Smurfs through a blender and slap the resulting liquid on the wall: that kind of blue.

The first thing they painted was a window frame. Watching open-mouthed from our offices, we told one another, "Maybe that's just the color of the woodwork." But then they started slapping paint on the brick walls and the stone trim and the iron railing around the little balcony. So we told one another, "Okay, it's probably just a primer, and the finish coat will be quieter." Ha. Fat chance. No paint manufacturer in the world would make a primer that color. This house was going to be all-blue and nothing but, from sidewalk to ridgepole.

Of the houses that flank Ol' Blue, one is painted a yellowish beige and the other a sort of taupe (a color, incidentally, that I swear didn't exist until a few years ago). These houses are handsome, but not eye-catching. They recede into the background, exuding genteel reti-

cence from every brick. By contrast, "reticence" is not a word that could be applied to the new (blue) kid on the block. Even on gloomy gray mornings, it was so supernaturally luminous that passersby stopped in their tracks when they first caught sight of it. On sunny days, the dazzling facade made the bluest sky look drab by comparison, and when a yellow car parked in front of it, you wanted to stand up and sing the Swedish national anthem.

This Major Blueness Event isn't the only happening in our neighborhood. Just around the corner, construction crews have been erecting the newest addition to our block of Massachusetts Avenue. The building, which houses The International Institute for Institutional Internationalism or something like that, is a miniature version of the curtain-wall skyscrapers that sprouted everywhere in the 1960s, all straight lines and sharp angles and sleek surfaces — but with subtle, deft design touches that lift it out of the ordinary. It's slightly cocky and surprisingly elegant.

It's also very different from its neighbors. Right next door is a Beaux-Arts townhouse built in 1906 for a wealthy coal-mining magnate who died six years later on the *Titanic*. Elsewhere on the block there are brick rowhouses, stripped-down Deco apartment buildings, and just about everything else. Now there's a cool glass box, too.

Some people don't care much for this newcomer, but I find it a welcome addition to the street. What's more, I also found myself getting downright fond of the blue apparition outside my window. That is, I was fond of it until some guys showed up one weekend (after a visit from the Color Police?) and repainted the whole house white — or off-white, actually, since that blue undercoat refuses to die quietly. The street seems much more placid now, and I'm feeling sort of let down.

In any vibrant neighborhood, new ingredients get added to the visual stew from time to time. This is a good thing. When an environment gets so tame that it's practically invisible, we need an elbow-jab in the ribs — a glass box or a splash of blue paint — to wake us up and make us pay attention, to remind us to keep our terminology straight. "Change" and "historic district" are not antithetical concepts. "Compatible" doesn't have to be a synonym for "bland." "Lively" isn't the same as "bad," and "startling" isn't necessarily a pejorative term, even in a historic district.

Besides, if life teaches us anything, it is that everything is temporary. Wait long enough, and new and outrageous gets old and familiar. Exotic strangers turn into members of the family. Tastes change, bright colors fade. And just when things settle back into routine, something new comes along to jab us in the ribs again — if we're lucky.

Looking good, glass box. As for you, Ol' Blue, the buzz was fun while it lasted.

PAST IMPERFECT

This replication business is getting way out of hand. Not the sheep-cloning thing, you understand; I can't seem to get worked up about that — although, having toiled on a ranch for a brief period in my youth, I do believe we already have all the sheep we need, thank you very much.

No, I'm talking about the replication of historic buildings and city skylines that threatens to drown the whole country in a sea of "Landmarks Lite."

Las Vegas has become a hotbed of this stuff. A few years ago, the opening of a hotel/casino called New York, New York brought to the Nevada desert a scaled-down version of the Manhattan skyline, with the Statue of Liberty and assorted skyscrapers all scrunched together and encircled by a roller coaster. Not far away, a new hotel that boasts replicas of Venice's Doge's Palace and St. Mark's Square will soon be joined by an even newer resort featuring knockoffs of the most famous landmarks of Paris. As if that weren't enough, there are plans to construct a miniature Grand Canyon with "60 tons of textured cast rock" in a nearby shopping mall. Elsewhere, there's a Leaning Tower of Pisa — complete with tilt — in Niles, Ill., while a Great Wall of China and a Forbidden City liven up the landscape in Kissimmee, Fla.

If this trend keeps up, foreign travel (travel to *real* foreign places, that is, not made-up ones) is bound to dwindle away to nothing. After all, why go all the way to Paris when you can see a perfectly good Eiffel Tower right here in the USA without having to put up with the funny money, smelly cheese, and relentless French-ness of the real City of Light? Why fly to India when you can drive to a Taj Mahal with clean rest rooms and a pretty decent golf course right next door?

An idea occurs to me. In their infinite wisdom, the city fathers in Reno, just up the road from Las Vegas, decided to demolish the historic Mapes Hotel a while back. Well, why don't we build a replica of the Mapes in Las Vegas? In fact, why don't we designate Las Vegas the Official Repository of the World's Worn-Out Cultural Heritage? It would be a fail-safe means of ensuring that treasured landmarks will live forever.

Worried that your favorite historic lighthouse might topple into the sea? Don't fret — we'll build another, better one here where it's nice and dry. There's plenty of room next door to the new Machu Picchu.

Still upset by the demolition of Penn Station? Relax — we'll replicate it right here. It'll be considerably smaller than the original, of course, but it'll have a casino and a wave pool.

Termites chewing up your historic district? Let 'em chomp — we'll build another one just like it (more or less) in termite-proof space-age polymers. I guarantee you'll like it better than the old historic district. That one was …well, *old*.

I can see the sign now, 20 stories of flashing, swooping neon:

HERITAGE,
HERE WHERE
IT'S HANDY
Plus the
Astounding
Siegfried and
Roy and the
World's Longest
Salad Bar

valet parking, and the attendants are dressed fetchingly in mini-togas) to gawk at a volcano that erupts at regular intervals, spewing rivers of fluorescent lava that smells like a piña colada, while the roller coaster clickety-clacks down the side of the Empire State Building. The plaintive tenor tones of a gondolier steering his craft past the Doge's Palace echo through the "textured cast rock" walls of the Grand Canyon, where the squeals of happy shoppers momentarily drown out the din of a million quarters sliding down the gullets of a thousand slot machines.

But that's a pipe dream. The present reality is gloriously goofy enough.

Picture me cruising down the Strip, stopping for a traffic light in front of a towering Egyptian pyramid and a medieval castle. At the Roman Forum I alight from my SUV (there's plenty of

Ah, brave new world indeed. C'mon, let's mosey over to Westminster Abbey for a burrito.

Speaking Volumes

One of the best things about the neighborhood where I work is that a five-minute walk will take me to a half-dozen different bookstores. The one I visit most frequently is a funky place where the aisles are narrow and the shelves are overstuffed and the air is thick with the musty, homey smell that emanates only from secondhand books. It is one of the best smells in the world.

When I first started accumulating books, I was interested only in brand-new ones. I loved the look of unwrinkled dust jackets and unsmudged pages, reveled in the smug feeling of being the first to open the cover and inhale the tang of ink and paper and glue fresh from the printer. But over the years my tastes have changed. Nowadays the books that appeal to me most are those that have most obviously belonged to someone else before me — the ones with intriguing blots and scribbled notes in an unfamiliar hand.

Take, for example, my secondhand copy of Henry James's *A Little Tour in France*, published in 1885. It's a handsome volume, with nicely marbled covers and a green leather spine stamped in gold. But what I like best about it is the fact that someone named "Margaret" bought it in Naples in 1921 (it says so right on the flyleaf) and car-

ried it around France, underlining passages and writing comments in the margins as she went. When James remarks that the Roman architecture of the Pont du Gard exhibits "a certain stupidity, a vague brutality," Margaret begs to differ: "He was no architect!" she writes in her precise hand. On another page, James's magisterial pronouncement that "the most charming thing at Poitiers is simply the Promenade de Blossac," leads Margaret to gush, "Yes yes yes yes," punctuating her endorsement with a thicket of exclamation marks.

Leafing through these pages, appreciating the fact that James's book is richer and livelier for having been Margaret's before it was mine, I realize that what makes secondhand books interesting is the same thing that makes old houses appealing: Passing through other people's hands has given them personality.

You can see it at Drayton Hall, the grand 18th-century house near Charleston, S.C. Visitors are shown a wealth of splendid architectural detail — fine brickwork, handsome carving, and decorative plaster — and most of them are properly awestruck. But when they're also shown century-old pencil marks on a doorframe that record the height of various Draytons (including a dog or two), suddenly they aren't awed anymore, they're smiling. The place has stopped being a Monument and become something better: *Real*.

One of the most enjoyable books I read last year was James Morgan's *If These Walls Had Ears*. It's a biography of Morgan's house in Little Rock — the story of the families who lived in it and the changes they made to it over a 60-year span. I don't know the names and histories of the people who lived in my home before me, but, like Morgan, I'm surrounded by the evidence of them. It's there in the stair treads worn down by the scuff of shoes outgrown and discarded decades ago, a record of a near-century of men and women and children going up the stairs to bed at night. Spotting these traces of a previous presence, like the jottings in the margins of a secondhand book, makes exploring an old building a treasure-hunt, makes living in an old house a daily communion with the past.

My last home was a rental apartment, so I didn't have the luxury of ripping out walls or repainting the woodwork — but I managed to leave my mark on it just the same. On my last morning there, after the movers had taken the furniture away and left me alone in the echoing rooms, I went into the bedroom closet and wrote on the sheetrock above the door, "Dwight Young lived happily in this apartment from 1/2/84 to 12/2/91." The inscription may go unnoticed for some time, but someday someone will spot it. They'll know I was there, and maybe (I hope) they'll think the place is better, richer, for it.

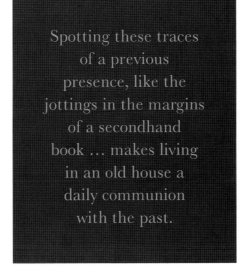

Spotting these traces of a previous presence, like the jottings in the margins of a secondhand book … makes living in an old house a daily communion with the past.

No Place Fast

I've been reading about a group called Slow Food, and what they're up to strikes me as a really good thing.

Born in Italy in response to the opening of a McDonald's restaurant in Rome's historic Piazza di Spagna in 1986, the Slow Food movement spread (slowly, I assume) across Europe until, in 1989, representatives from 20 countries met in Paris and issued a manifesto. "We are enslaved by speed," they proclaimed, "and have all succumbed to the same insidious virus: Fast Life…." Bemoaning the fact that Fast Life "has changed our way of being and threatens our environment and our landscapes," they urged that "our defense should begin at the table with Slow Food. Let us rediscover the flavors and savors of regional cooking…."

(At last: a movement to which I can devote every ounce of my being, not to mention every notch on my belt!)

Slow Food has now spawned Slow Cities, a network of communities (all of them in Italy as of now, but they hope to enlist members all over the world) committed to creating and maintaining "an identity of their own that is visible outside and profoundly felt inside." Slow Cities pledge, among other things, to "implement an environmental policy…placing the onus on recovery and reuse techniques," to "imple-ment an infrastructural policy which is functional for the improvement, not the occupation, of the land" and to "promote the quality of hospitality as a real bond with the local community." In other words, they'll try to keep a grip on what makes them unique, and encourage everyone to drop by and enjoy it.

(Note to Slow Cities: If you're looking for a poster-child, I'm your boy. I'm willing to work — the more slowly the better — for food, particularly of the Italian variety.)

The Slow Food movement's symbol is the snail, a creature to which I've been feeling a certain degree of kinship. You see, on an otherwise unremarkable Sunday morning last July, I fell off a ladder and broke my leg. The accident put me in a cast for several weeks and on crutches for several more, and I became a slow walker.

Before that fateful — nay, cataclysmic — July morning I generally moved along at a pretty fast clip. I rarely strolled, almost never dawdled. Decidedly unsnail-like, that was me. Nowadays, by contrast, I saunter as if born to it, and I find that I'm seeing things I never noticed before.

Like the animals, for instance. In my neighborhood there's a block of Victorian rowhouses that are a-crawl with critters — squirrels and owls mostly, all carved with great precision in the brownstone lintels and keystones. I've passed those houses a thousand times, but I never saw the carved animals until recently — and now I'm seeing them everywhere. Near my office there's a turn-of-the-century apartment house that turns out to have elephants under the first-floor windowsills. And just the other day I spotted a particularly ferocious dragon (at least I think it's a dragon, though it could be a salamander with attitude) glaring down from the eaves of an embassy up the street.

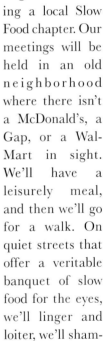

There's other stuff, too: a delicate fanlight here, some mellow old brickwork there *(Ladies and gentlemen, a round of applause, if you please, for the ever-lovely Flemish bond with glazed headers!)*, even something as fleeting — and deeply satisfying — as the shadow of winter branches on a creamy clapboard wall. These things have been there all along,

but I never noticed them until a gimpy leg shunted me to the slow lane of "Fast Life." Who knew that moving at a snail's pace could be so enlightening?

So now I'm thinking about forming a local Slow Food chapter. Our meetings will be held in an old neighborhood where there isn't a McDonald's, a Gap, or a Wal-Mart in sight. We'll have a leisurely meal, and then we'll go for a walk. On quiet streets that offer a veritable banquet of slow food for the eyes, we'll linger and loiter, we'll shamble and slouch, we'll lollygag and dillydally. In short, we'll celebrate, with suitably languorous lentitude, the joys of slowing down.

FLICKS ALFRESCO

One of these days I'm going to drive up to Camden, N.J., — not to visit the Walt Whitman house or the Campbell Soup Company's museum of antique soup tureens, although I'm sure both are well worth the trip, but to see if there's a historic marker at the birthplace of the drive-in movie theater.

On any list of Great American Inventions, the drive-in has to appear near the top — up there with cheeseburgers and Barcaloungers. Given the fact that it combines our national love of cars, movies, and informality, the drive-in probably was an inevitability — but it took one Richard M. Hollingshead to make it happen. In his driveway, Hollingshead experimented with some home movies and a radio until he was satisfied that it was possible to see and hear a movie from a car. In May of 1933 he patented a system of ramps that angled the front of each car upward, assuring everyone a clear view of the screen. A few weeks later, on June 6, the Automobile Movie Theater opened for business in Camden with more than 600 people in attendance. There were some bugs to be worked out — sound from screen-mounted speakers was sometimes inaudible to patrons in the back rows and all too audible to residents of nearby houses — but the idea was a hit.

Within a couple of decades, more than 5,000 drive-ins were lighting up the nocturnal landscape.

Don and Susan Sanders relate this history in a terrific book called *The American Drive-In Movie Theatre* (Motorbooks International, 1997). It traces the development of technological refinements and amenities — such as the squawky speaker boxes that hung on the car window and the puny heaters that plugged into the cigarette lighter; the playgrounds where kids, many of them dressed in pajamas, could work off excess energy before the movie started; and the snack bars whose belly-busting wares were hawked on the screen by dancing wieners and grinning Milk Duds. It's an unabashedly nostalgic celebration of all the Sunsets and Starlites and Skyvues that flourished and withered in such a short span of time.

Photos in the book remind us that at many drive-ins a neon display or painted mural turned the back of the giant screen into a roadside work of art. On the screen itself, however, art was in short supply. The drive-in was never a venue for Serious Cinema, being much more likely to showcase something in the *Bongo Beach Bikini Bimbo* genre or — my own personal favorite — the Dusk-to-Dawn Monsterthon. For my friends and me, trips to the drive-in for an all-night parade of blood-sucking slime creatures, giant ants, and city-wrecking atomic-mutant lizards were a staple of adolescence. At least once a month we'd pile into someone's car for a night-long orgy of gloriously bad movies, punctuated by frequent trips to the snack bar for chili dogs and fries and sodas and candy. By the time the last monster was vanquished just before daybreak, we were cranky and scratchy-eyed from sleeplessness and woozy with indigestion...and ready to do it all over again in a couple of weeks.

Back then there were a half-dozen drive-ins in my hometown. The last one to open had two huge screens — a sure sign, we thought, of the continuing evolution of man's genius and a harbinger of things to come. We were wrong: Within a few years, the spread of multiscreen theaters, the advent of the VCR, and the disappearance of cars big enough to loll in made the drive-in a dinosaur.

But it isn't extinct. According to the Sanders' book, about 500 are still in business across the country — in many cases not merely hanging on but thriving. I've heard about one near Baltimore where they begin each evening's performance with "The Star-Spangled Banner." When the music strikes up, patrons stand beside their cars and sing. And after the last note fades away, amid a great slamming of doors and slurping of sodas, the movie begins.

It sounds like a fine way to spend an evening. I'm dying to experience it for myself, but one thing worries me. I know I'll get all choked up — and a lump in your throat is not something you want when you've got a foot-long chili dog staring you in the face.

UPDATE: Drive-ins have lots of fans, and that has led to the creation of several interesting and informative websites. A good starting point is www.driveinmovie.com ("made from 100% real Americana, natural nostalgia and fresh pulp"), which has an invaluable state-by-state listing of surviving theaters. Others include: www.drive-ins.com, www.drivein-theater.com, and www.driveinworkshop.com, which includes tips and technical info for those who want to open a drive-in of their very own.

By the way, I still don't know whether there's a historic marker at the birthplace of the drive-in — but I do know that the Campbell Soup Company's soup-tureen collection is no longer in Camden, N.J. It's now permanently housed at Winterthur, the former home of Henry Francis du Pont near Wilmington, Del.

Soul-Lifting Cities

Recently I was watching *The Time Machine*, the 1960 film in which Rod Taylor builds a device that enables him to travel across centuries. Predictably, Something Goes Horribly Wrong. Hurled into the distant future, he finds that mankind has evolved into two races: the Morlocks, who are inarticulate, cannibalistic, and exceedingly homely; and the Eloi, dim-bulb Barbie and Ken dolls wearing little pastel tunics.

Toward the end of the movie, as it became apparent that the Morlocks weren't going to eat all of the Eloi as I had hoped, I found myself wondering where I'd choose to go if I had a time machine. Not into the future; too many unforeseeables. Not too far into the past, either — no dinosaurs for me, thanks. No, I believe I'd want to be set down in Chicago, on a sunny morning in 1893, at the World's Columbian Exposition.

At the Chicago fair, Americans saw what could be achieved when truly creative minds were entrusted with planning and shaping the urban environment. Working in close collaboration, giants like Daniel H. Burnham, Richard Morris Hunt, Frederick Law Olmsted, and Augustus Saint-Gaudens created the dream-like White City, where buildings, mostly neoclassical in style and with a uniform cornice height, were artfully sited along waterways and broad avenues

dotted with sculpture and plantings. The millions who saw or heard about these dazzling structures and breathtaking vistas became fascinated with the possibility of transforming the hodgepodge of their hometowns into something more like the fair's vision of harmony and orderliness. The seeds of the City Beautiful movement were planted, to blossom eventually in scattered enclaves of great dignity and beauty — places like Philadelphia's Benjamin Franklin Parkway and the civic centers of San Francisco and Cleveland.

Handsome as they are, these places are just pieces of the dream. I want to go to the source, the White City itself. I want to wander around the Court of Honor, where a vast pool reflected the gleam of white-columned facades. I want to hear the fountains splash, the flags snap. Most of all I want to see Daniel Chester French's statue of *The Republic*, a 65-foot-high gilded image of idealized womanhood dressed in classical robes, her arms raised as if blessing the towers and domes that surround her.

Some critics say the White City was a too-carefully orchestrated stage-set, a pastiche of outmoded forms that retarded the progress of modern architecture for a generation. But for me, the fair and its era represent a golden age when planners, architects, artists, and craftsmen pooled their talents to produce works of genius that carried America into a new century. That century is ending now, and it seems we've forgotten the lessons learned from the fair's lofty experiment in urban design.

We're left with cities that we make excuses for. "It's a true urban environment — really gritty," we say, when what we mean is that the windows are boarded up and the walls are splashed with graffiti. "Living here has an exhilarating edge to it," we say, when what we mean is that our senses are bombarded by traffic noise and exhaust fumes and our spirits are numbed by architecture that is rarely inspiring and mostly banal. "This is no theme park," we say, "this place is *real*," when what we mean is that it's poorly planned, haphazardly developed, and visually chaotic.

Pressed for a description of contemporary landmarks, we spout cold statistics: "It's bigger than 20 football fields," we say, or, "It cost more than 100 million dollars." What we *can't* say truthfully — not very often, at any rate — is, "It's beautiful."

> I want to experience... that all-too-brief moment when it seemed only reasonable to think that cities could be — *should be* — beautiful.

I want an urban environment that works well and looks good. I need safe streets and efficient traffic-handling, of course, but I also need my soul lifted once in a while. What I want is the fulfillment of the Chicago fair's glorious promise.

Failing that, I want to experience, in the place where millions of others experienced it, that all-too-brief moment when it seemed only reasonable to think that cities could be — *should be* — beautiful. What I really need in my life right now is a glimpse of the sunlight flashing on that gilded statue of a lovely woman, her serene image reflected in a still pool, her arms uplifted in benediction.

UPDATE: A scaled-down version of *The Republic*, about one-third the size of the original, stands in Chicago's Jackson Park, the site of the 1893 fair. Not far away, the imposing Museum of Science and Industry is a replica of the fair's Palace of Fine Arts.

THE RECENT PASSED

Last weekend I spent a couple of hours leafing through a somewhat unsettling book called *Going, Going, Gone*. It's all about change — not high-level stuff like The Rise of the Mercantile Class or The Fall of the Hohenzollern Dynasty, but more mundane matters like the disappearance of carbon paper. The premise of authors Susan Jonas and Marilyn Nissenson is simple and startling: A whole host of things that we delighted in or took for granted or even depended on *just yesterday* have gone the way of the dinosaur or are on the verge of doing so.

Admittedly, some vanished things we're better off without. Polio scares, slide rules, and girdles, for instance: Don't need 'em, don't miss 'em. Others, however, are eminently missable: Soda fountains. Penmanship. Etiquette.

The whole thing has me a bit rattled, especially since I've realized that this process of gradual extinction is making inroads in the fields of architecture and urban design.

Consider, for example, what's happening to downtown pedestrian malls: They're disappearing, that's what. Once hailed as the last, best hope for saving Main Street, downtown malls were as ubiquitous as bell-bottoms in the 1970s. But now that they've fallen out of favor, look at what's happening in town after town: They're uprooting all those trees with little tiny light bulbs in the branches. They're getting rid of the space-age street lamps and the concrete tubs with dead geraniums or alien-looking ornamental cabbages in them. And horror of horrors, they're welcoming the cars back.

(A brief digression: I remember one town — I believe it was in Louisiana — where the long-closed street was reopened by the simple expedient of taking down the barriers and letting the cars in. The result was livelier than anyone intended, since a drive down Main Street meant negotiating a tricky slalom of benches, fountains, planters, and chess tables — not to mention bench sitters and chess players. City fathers soon realized their mistake and ripped out all of the street furniture, but locals still speak wistfully of those few heady days when a downtown drive was more fun than a ride on the county fair's Dodge-'em Cars.)

It's not just the malls that are disappearing. The overhead walkways are coming down, too — at least in Baltimore. A recent editorial in *The Baltimore Sun* hailed the demolition of the "forbidding concrete terrace and skywalks" at a state office complex as an "urban landscape miracle." That's quite a change from the days when vertical separation of traffic — pedestrians

Voyages

upstairs, cars downstairs, subways in the basement, and snazzy glass-walled elevators connecting all the levels — was a hallmark of modern urban planning. If the current revisionist trend continues, people all over the country will be reduced to walking on ground-level sidewalks again, and the world-of-tomorrow skywalk will be as rare and quaint as the rotary-dial telephone.

By the same token, an alarmist might worry about the survival of yesterday's architecture of tomorrow. Among the landmarks pictured in a 1965 guide to Washington, D.C., architecture is the Longfellow Building, designed by William Lescaze in 1940 and described as "Washington's first modern office building." The building still stands, but it doesn't look like the photo in the guidebook anymore. A major makeover a few years ago softened the cantilevered balconies and hard planes that made the building a paradigm of the International Style, and a more recent remodeling gave the street-level storefronts a demure veneer of neoclassicism that

> With the demise of so many glass boxes, it's not inconceivable that future architectural historians will conclude that the 1950s and 60s never happened.

probably would have horrified Lescaze.

Similar facelifts happened all over the country during the heyday of post-modernism a decade ago. Sleek curtain-wall facades, emblematic of architecture's break with historicism, were removed or slipcovered in a pseudo-historical pastiche of columns, cornices, and Palladian windows. With the demise of so many glass boxes, it's not inconceivable that future architectural historians will conclude that the 1950s and 60s never happened.

So what am I to make of this rampant revamping of the not-so-old urban scene? I could tell myself that this stuff was ugly, ill-conceived, and shoddily built to start with, and we're well rid of it — but hasn't that argument been used to justify the demolition of many good buildings in the past? I could gird up my loins and fight to save these things — but does that mean we have to preserve *everything*?

I'm not sure how I ought to feel. I'd take a walk and think it over, but I'm afraid of getting beaned by a piece of the recent past. There's a lot of it falling.

REAL REELS

In flickering images on the screen, blacksmiths pound away at an anvil. They pause, mop their brows, and start to work again. Oddly, the impact of their hammers makes no sound; the silence of the theater is broken only by the distant whir of the projector. A few seconds later, the film ends.

This one-minute snippet represents the motion picture at its most elemental: no soundtrack, no big-name stars, no special effects. Dating from 1893, it was the first film exhibited commercially in the United States. Now it's an orphan.

A few decades ago, much of America's cinematic heritage was headed for oblivion. Carelessly stored, unstable film stock was disintegrating, reducing vibrant images to lifeless dust. Many films — including works by important directors and actors — had simply vanished, consigned to the trash pile or the incinerator because there seemed to be no reason to save them.

Fortunately, the growth of cable TV and the advent of the VCR led to the development of new markets for old films, and preservation efforts were stepped up. Today, the legacy of the Hollywood dream factories is in much better shape than it was a quarter-century ago, and new generations of viewers can appreciate the work of silent-era pioneers, plumb the shadowy depths of

film noir cynicism, and revel in the jaw-dropping excesses of MGM musicals.

But our motion-picture heritage is more than timeless masterworks and big-budget extravaganzas. Museums, libraries, and archives all over the country shelter another class of film treasures, rarely seen and largely unknown to even the most ardent buffs. These are orphan films — little-known silents, documentaries, experimental shorts, advertising and training films, even home movies — for which there is no established commercial market and little economic incentive for preservation. Saving them is part of the mission of the National Film Preservation Foundation.

Created in 1996 and affiliated with the Library of Congress, NFPF has worked with dozens of archives (most recently through the Save America's Treasures program) to identify orphan films, preserve them, and make them available to a wider public. Recent screenings in several cities and a DVD anthology titled "Treasures of American Film Archives" showcase a few of the wonders they've uncovered — and what an incredibly varied, endearingly wacky, and staggeringly important collection it is.

Some of the films have genuine historical significance. A 1924 silent melodrama called *The Chechahcos* is laughably bad for the most part, with hammy actors chewing up the scenery right and left. But occasionally there's a scene — a dogsled moving across a vast snowfield, for instance — to remind us that this was the first feature film shot (with considerable difficulty) in Alaska.

Other orphans with no such claim to fame are no less interesting. There are newsreel outtakes that serve up jolting doses of firsthand history. There are documentaries that flash engaging vignettes of life as it used to be: An amateur effort from Minnesota shows farmers scything their fields and neighbors sharing a beer in the tavern, and a "community portrait" of a West Virginia town includes local churchgoers posing in their stiff collars and formidable hats. And there are some fascinating home movies, ranging from footage of Japanese-American families struggling to adjust to conditions in their World War II internment camp to a sunnier vision of domestic life in which Groucho Marx clowns around as he sees his children off to school.

Is any of these a potential box-office blockbuster? Nope.

Are they worth saving? Absolutely.

These orphan films are important pages in America's 20th-century family album, and saving them is essential to our continued ability to know who we are and how we got this way. By ensuring that these films won't be lost, NFPF offers us a chance to get a new look at the most fascinating cinematic subject of all: ourselves in full glorious flower, noble and innocent and proud and completely nuts, all decked out in strange clothes and weird hairstyles.

Look, up there on the screen. That's us. Don't we look funny? Don't we look fine? And isn't it good to have these pictures to remember us by?

UPDATE: For more information on the work of the National Film Preservation Foundation — and to view clips from a few of the more than 525 orphan films that have been saved — visit the NFPF website: www.filmpreservation.org.

CHISELINGS

I've been reading a book called *Public Sculpture in New Jersey* — admittedly not the sort of title that sets the pulse racing, but a fascinating book nonetheless. Who knew that the Garden State had such a wealth of sculpture? I didn't, but now, thanks to this handsomely illustrated volume, I do.

It's no surprise that New Jersey boasts plenty of frock-coated portrait statues — from James A. Bradley, who founded Asbury Park, to James A. Garfield, who died in Long Branch — and the usual run of stone and bronze memorials to the war dead. What is surprising is the state's rich collection of sculpture that addresses themes of a somewhat *quirkier* nature.

In Ocean City, for example, a drinking fountain for dogs displays an endearing portrait of Hobo, a stray pooch who was rescued from a snowdrift in 1920 and became the town's unofficial mascot. A bronze relief in West Windsor Township commemorates Orson Welles's 1938 "War of the Worlds" radio broadcast, which panicked millions of people into believing that America had been invaded by Martians. And a monument in Haddonfield pays tribute to the 1858 discovery of the skeleton of *Hadrosaurus foulkii*, New Jersey's official State Dinosaur. Who knew?

By coincidence, *Public Sculpture in New Jersey* came into my hands shortly after I'd finished reading another, equally fascinating book called *Public Sculpture in Wisconsin*. As you'd expect, the streets, parks, and public squares of Wisconsin are populated with the same rich variety of monuments as those of New Jersey — with a notable addition: chainsaw art. From a colorful portrait of Willie Nelson in Hurley to a clutch of trolls in Mount Horeb, the work of chainsaw carvers enlivens the landscape all over the state. In fact, judging from the number of logs that have been buzz-cut into sculpture, Wisconsin must be littered with piles of sawdust big enough to be seen from the moon — or at least Minnesota.

I've always been a great fan of outdoor sculpture — and it's a good thing, because I live now in a city in which it's practically impossible to walk more than two blocks without bumping into a statue of a general spurring a horse or a politician striking a pose.

Almost every one of them offers something interesting or moving or surprising to look at. Among my personal favorites is a memorial to Dr. Samuel Hahnemann (who? the father of homeopathy, that's who) which is graced with one of the most beautiful mosaic panels I've ever seen. I'm also very fond of a marble Indian in front of Union Station; he's gazing off toward the Capitol dome, and I'd love to know what he's thinking.

But there's more to these monuments than artistic merit or even simple visual appeal. They're important (this is going to sound obvious, but give me a minute) because of the messages they convey. They exist because someone thought, *This thing — this lovable stray dog, this battle, this woman who did good works, even this invasion from Mars that never really happened — this is worth remembering.*

Every monument, every statue, every plaque nudges us gently (and sometimes not so gently) in the ribs and whispers, "Don't lose this. It's important. It may be just a tiny piece of the outside edge of the puzzle, but without it, the picture — the vast, many-layered, multicolored portrait of who we are, how we got here, what we went through — isn't really complete." It's a voice we need to pay attention to.

With this in mind, I'm laying plans for a road trip. You can hie yourself off to Bali or Bechuanaland if you want to, but I'm itching to go to New Jersey for a look at that War of the Worlds Memorial. And then I may just head for Green Lake, Wisc., to stroll through the Gloria Hills Sculpture Garden, which the book describes as an "Art Environment" featuring (fasten your seat belts) more than 50 "giant fish, embellished cars, instrument en-

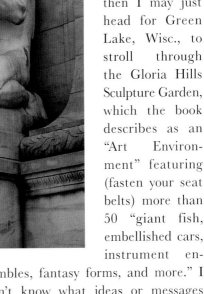

sembles, fantasy forms, and more." I don't know what ideas or messages these things convey, but judging from the photographs, it's a totally wacked-out and wonderful place — and who knows what treasures lurk in that tantalizing "and more"?

The Mellow Brick Mode

When they get around to com-piling the definitive anthol-ogy of the best song lyrics of all time, I'm sure these lines from the Eagles' "Take It Easy" will be included:

Well I'm a-standin' on a corner in
Winslow, Arizona,
Such a fine sight to see:
It's a girl, my Lord,
In a flat-bed Ford
Slowin' down to take a look at me.

Sheer poetry, that's what it is — espe-cially that "girl my Lord/flat-bed Ford" couplet, which I consider the equal of just about anything Shakespeare ever wrote.

A while back, I was actually in Winslow, Ariz., where I was delighted to learn of the existence of an outfit called the Standin' on the Corner Foundation. The foundation's mission is to create the — what else? — Standin' on the Corner Park, located smack in the mid-dle of town on historic Route 66, right on the very corner (presumably) that the Eagles sang about. I'm not sure how long the project has been underway, but they've already made considerable progress. There's a fine mural in place, showing the fabled flat-bed Ford with the aforementioned girl behind the steering wheel, and there's a bronze statue of a guy doing just what you'd expect: a-standin' on the corner.

And how is the foundation paying for all this? By selling bricks, that's how. A check for $50 buys the donor a 4" x 8" brick with a 3-line inscription of his or her choosing. For the inscription-ally challenged, the foundation's web-site offers some suggestions: "In mem-ory of J.F. Kennedy" or "To my girl Winona" or "Always takin' it easy Fred Tasmoni." (Fred, I'm sure you'll agree, has the right idea.)

It can't have escaped your notice that inscribed bricks are taking over the world. It's getting so you can't walk any-where without stepping on bricks that pay tribute to "The Mitchell Family 1999" or proclaim things like "Always in our hearts John Lennon." I must admit that my initial opinion of these things was that their position on the evolution-ary ladder was just one step above graf-fiti. "Fools' names and fools' faces… something something… public places," I'd mutter to myself, grinning loftily whenever I noted that a passerby had deposited a particularly nasty bit of lit-ter on a brick named Earl or Eunice.

But I've mellowed. Now I think these personalized pavers are a good thing. They represent an endearingly human bid for what the Winslow foundation describes as "a piece of immortality." Let's face it: The state of the world being what it is, the perennially laid-back

Fred Tasmoni may never have a statue erected to him — but at least he has a brick with his name on it, and with any luck that brick is going to last a long time. What's more (and more important), his brick is in a place that has meaning for him, a place that resonates inside him in a way that he — perhaps only he — knows and holds close.

We all need something like that. I've concluded that at age 50, everyone should be issued a set of bricks inscribed with his or her name. You get to decide where to install your bricks, but you want to make sure each one goes to the *right* place — a house or street about which you want to say, This brick with my name on it shows that I own a piece of this place, and it owns a piece of me too.

You might decide to put one of your bricks in Winslow, Ariz. One of mine would go to Eutaw, Ala. There's a big old house there called Kirkwood where I once visited some friends named Swayze. There was a full moon that night, so it just seemed natural to sit in rocking chairs out on the porch for a while, and then it just seemed natural that someone would show up with a guitar. Of course we wound up singing old songs to the moon.

It was such a fine sight to see, that moon. Probably worthy of an Eagles song. Definitely worth a brick.

UPDATE: The foundation's website, www.standinonthecorner.com, offers information on the park. It also offers a wide variety of merchandise for sale — everything from "Standin' on a Corner" t-shirts and refrigerator magnets to the aforementioned inscribed bricks. You can order all of these things on the internet, of course, but it would be much more fun to go to Winslow and shop in person. If you go, you should definitely check out La Posada, a recently restored hotel designed by Mary Jane Colter for the Fred Harvey Company in 1929.

One more thing: Several readers reprimanded me for not crediting Jackson Browne for writing "Take It Easy." Point taken — but for me it'll always be an Eagles song.

SWEET SHELTER

My house sits near the end of a block of 11 rowhouses. Stretching to the right and left from my front door is a long vista of near-identical porches. Kids play on them. Adults read the paper on them. Flags, flowers, and "For Rent" signs adorn them. On rainy days, mail carriers step over the railings from one porch to the next and make their deliveries without getting wet. You get the idea: A porch is a good thing.

When I say "porch," I mean front porch. A back porch is something else altogether. A back porch is where you can, if you're of a mind to do so, take out the garbage in your underwear. A front porch, on the other hand, is where you spend time doing things that are good for you: hangin' out, chattin', watchin' the world go by. (One of the best things about a porch is the fact that a final "g" seems totally out of place there.)

We Americans certainly didn't invent the porch, but over time we refined it and turned it into something that, perhaps more than any other architectural feature, is quintessentially American. I mean, what's more American than Mount Vernon? And when you look at a picture of Mount Vernon, what do you see? A great big white-pillared porch, that's what — although I believe George Washington may have called it a piazza.

Washington was ahead of his time in stretching a porch across the front of his house. For the most part, porches in the late 18th and early 19th centuries were pretty puny things, functioning mostly to keep the rain off your head while you fumbled for your door key or waited for your host to answer your knock. Our national love affair with the porch didn't really go into high gear until the second quarter of the 19th century, when the Romantic Movement swept through and taught us that Nature was something to be enjoyed, not avoided.

Combining the best features of indoors and outdoors, a porch was the perfect place from which to gaze upon, and interact with, the wide, wonderful world. Practically overnight, porches got big enough to have furniture on them: From coast to coast, rocking chairs creaked, plant stands groaned under the weight of ferns and aspidistra, and porch swings staked their claim to the title of Best Invention Ever. Firmly established as an essential fixture of American social life, the porch briefly sent a cooling breeze through the stuffy chambers of politics when William McKinley conducted most of his 1896 presidential campaign from his Ohio front porch — a fact that leads to the inescapable conclusion that he may have been the smartest candidate in history.

In the 1950s and 60s, they fell out of fashion: Postwar suburban houses didn't have porches, they had air conditioning and patios. But now they're back: In the so-called "New Urbanism" communities that have sprung up in recent years — Seaside, Fla., is probably the best known — almost every house has a porch. That's cause for celebration, especially now that summertime is here.

Some years ago I learned that "porch" can be a verb as well as a noun. One warm day I overheard a passerby call out "How y'all doin'?" to some of my neighbors who were sitting in front of their house, enjoying the late-afternoon breeze. Their languid reply was, "We're fine. We're just sittin' here porchin'."

Go and do likewise. Find a porch (or a piazza or veranda, if that's what's handy — but not a stoop, which is what houses had before they grew porches, and don't think for a minute that a deck is the same thing), settle into something comfortable (it's nice if there's a rail to prop your feet on, but if not, you'll definitely need a footstool), wrap your hand around a glass with ice and something else in it, and read Michael Dolan's *The American Porch: An Informal History of an Informal Place* (Lyons Press, 2002). It'll make you grateful for the unsung hero who first realized that a place for porchin' is the blessedly breeze-washed bedrock of a civilized society.

TRUE GRIT

While I was in graduate school I worked briefly on an archeological dig in Virginia. It was midsummer. The heat was murderous — and so were the humidity, the ticks, the granite-hard layer of marl that I had to hack through, and the smell from a nearby sewage treatment plant. The experience taught me two valuable lessons: (1) profanity is therapeutic, and (2) archeology is hard.

You can see why I have such respect for the students who took part in this summer's 14th annual archeology field school at Montpelier.

I visited the site recently with the Trust's senior archeologist Lynne Lewis, who has a more extensive and intimate knowledge of National Trust dirt than just about anybody else. Lewis showed me through the archeology lab, where a couple of students were picking through little mounds of soil and gravel, peering through magnifying glasses and sorting their finds into piles of snail shells, plant material, and pottery fragments. Then we went out to take a look at the site of this year's dig: a corner of the Montpelier acreage called Mount Pleasant, where Ambrose and Frances Madison, President James Madison's grandparents, first settled in 1732.

Letters and other documents have already taught us a good deal about life at Mount Pleasant. An inventory of Ambrose Madison's estate, for instance, tallies the number of livestock and books and pieces of furniture that he owned. (Unless I'm misinterpreting something, these statistics indicate that almost every sheep on the place had a book and a chair — evidence that life on the 18th-century Virginia frontier was both more bizarre and more genteel than we think.)

But documents can't tell us everything. We want to know not just how much tax these long-ago Madisons paid, but what kind of food they ate; not just how many slaves worked these fields, but what kind of clothes they wore and what kinds of tools they used; not just who lived here, but how they lived. That's where archeology comes in.

This summer's dig turned up some broken wine bottles and other odds and ends, plus lots of what might be charitably described as detritus: tiny bits of bone, seeds, and charcoal. This brings up an important point. Much about archeology — from the Greek *archae* ("scratching in the dirt under a broiling sun") + *ology* ("instead of sitting in a cool room having a nice glass of iced tea with lemon") — can seem pretty unexciting to anyone but an archeologist. In fact, if you want to make an archeologist go all flinty-eyed, just ask, "Did you find any neat stuff?" When an 18th-century cuff-link was excavated this summer, the diggers passed it around and murmured the requisite ooohs and aaahs — but they've been known to get equally enthusiastic over the discovery of a fragment of brick or an odd stain in the soil. Clearly, the definition of "neat stuff" is very broad.

They still haven't found the main house site at Mount Pleasant. They thought they had it this year, but what they uncovered turned out to be an outbuilding. Nobody seemed disappointed. They know the main house is out there somewhere (in fact, Lewis already has her eye on a likely spot), and there'll be more students to help look for it next summer.

In the meantime, there's plenty to do. Earlier this year at Montpelier a film crew wanted to turn a herd of pigs loose in a pasture, so a pre-pig investigation of the site had to be carried out before the porkers' rooting disturbed any archeological evidence the soil might contain. Similar archeological rescue efforts are triggered by the digging of new septic fields and the construction of new parking lots at National Trust sites all over the country, and Lewis is on hand for most of them.

So the dirt flies and our knowledge grows. Every room at the Montpelier archeology lab is lined with shelves, and every shelf holds rows of cardboard boxes. In every box are carefully labeled paper bags, and every paper bag is filled with smaller plastic bags. And in every plastic bag are dozens of tiny windows into a vanished world.

UPDATE: In the summer of 2001, archeologists found the site of Ambrose and Frances Madison's house at Mount Pleasant. It was pretty much where Lynne Lewis thought it would be. The following year, they excavated the cellar of the house. The fact that they unearthed very few household remains (the student team's report notes the discovery of "a pile of charred peaches") probably indicates that the house had been stripped of usable materials before it burned sometime in the 1770s.

Plans for future years call for excavation of several features in the vicinity of the house site, including a ditch that promises to contain "dense deposits of trash material." I'm sure the diggers will have fun with that one: If there's one thing guaranteed to gladden the heart of an archeologist, it's a trash pit.

SEEING IT, SAVING IT

I have no idea who these people are. I found the photo on the sidewalk, picked it up out of curiosity, and haven't been able to throw it away.

I don't know their names, but I think I know a bit about them. They are Dad and the kids, squirming and squinting while Mom snaps the picture. They're sitting on the marble steps of the Lincoln Memorial, facing east toward the Washington Monument and the Capitol dome. Judging from their clothes, it's summer, about 25 years ago. They are on vacation.

Here's what I wonder: Do these children — wherever they are, whatever they've become — do they remember this trip? Did it change them, or change the world for them, in any way?

Asked when and how they first got interested in preservation, lots of people answer that it began in childhood, with trips to restored plantations, forts, and presidential birthplaces. When I hear that, I always feel that I missed out. During my own childhood, family vacations took us either to East Texas, where we visited relatives, or to Colorado or New Mexico, where we looked at mountains. History played no part in our travel plans.

My first intimation of the connection between history and place didn't come until much later, when I moved to

Richmond, Va. By then, I had been a history buff for many years, and in Richmond, for the first time in my life, I was confronted with tangible elements of the history that up to then had existed for me only in books. It was a life-changing revelation.

One morning I drove out to the battlefield at Beaver Dam Creek, the site of fierce fighting during the Seven Days campaign that raged around Richmond in the summer of 1862. I stood there with a guidebook in my hand...and I could see it. Right here — right next to this mound where I was standing — were the Union trenches. And over there was the hillside where the Confederates had charged out of the woods, running down the slope to the creek, firing their rifles and yelling in the summer heat. I could see it all. It was real.

Another day I went to St. Paul's Church downtown and, after a few minutes of searching, found the pew I was looking for. I sat in it and thought: This is where Jefferson Davis was sitting on that Sunday morning in 1865 when someone crept in and told him that Petersburg had fallen and Richmond was doomed. Right in this building. Here on this very spot.

The fact that I could see and walk through these places, could touch the nicks and grooves where history had bumped against them, impressed me enormously. It still does. In fact, the more I think about it, the more I'm convinced that this is one of the most important reasons why we choose to preserve old buildings and neighborhoods: These places permit us to have *tactile* encounters with the past. History stops being just an idea, a scrap of story, or a page in a book, and is transformed into a *thing* with texture and solidity — a brick wall, an iron railing, a pane of glass, a grassy trench, a church pew. Something you can connect with. Something you can touch.

> History stops being just an idea, a scrap of story, or a page in a book, and is transformed into a *thing* with texture and solidity — a brick wall, an iron railing, a pane of glass, a grassy trench, a church pew.

President's Box just to the right of the stage. And then maybe they walked across 10th Street to the Petersen House and looked into the tiny bedroom where Lincoln died. And maybe, just maybe, one of these kids — probably the oldest one — took it all in and realized: This is where history happened. Right here. And now I'm here too. I'm part of it.

If that happened — as it does to someone, somewhere, almost every day — this kid, who hated sitting still to have his picture taken, had a better vacation than he knew.

It didn't happen to me until I was an adult, but for some people — the lucky ones — the door opens much sooner.

Who knows? Maybe, on that day 25 years ago when this picture was taken, this nameless family went over to Ford's Theatre and saw the flag-draped

CHEERS

I recently came across a picture I took years ago on some small-town Main Street. It shows the upper floors of a 19th-century commercial building. Half of the facade is enlivened by ranks of regularly spaced windows and handsome (though somewhat scabby-looking) brickwork. On the other half, everything — brickwork, windows, cornice — is hidden behind an ugly skin of corrugated aluminum panels.

What makes the picture intriguing is that I can't remember whether I took it as that metal slipcover was being installed or as it was being dismantled in preparation for a long-overdue rehab. In other words, I can't remember whether this is a picture of bad news or good news.

That's the way it is when you work in preservation: Sometimes you can't tell whether you're winning or losing. But as we start a new year and draw closer to the start of a new millennium, I favor the former.

I'm convinced that preservationists are entitled to some self-administered pats on the back. Over the past few decades we've made a real difference in the way American communities look and in the way Americans value the evidence of the past. I don't want to paint too rosy a picture, but I believe we have much to feel good about. We haven't won yet — not by a long shot — but I think we're winning.

On your next road trip, slip off the interstate and drive through some towns. I've done it, and here's what I learned: It's hard to find an older residential neighborhood or business district that doesn't show signs of preservation's influence. In town after town, old houses that once languished like inmates on an architectural death row now sport new roofs and porches and paint jobs. You get the distinct impression that their owners are proud of these houses; they're not just biding their time until they can replace them with something newer.

It's the same story on almost every Main Street: Turn-of-the-century storefronts haven't looked this good since the turn of the century, with brickwork carefully repointed, long-overlooked architectural details highlighted, long-gone cornices and awnings replaced, and entire facades stripped of midcentury camouflage. Maybe too many of the stores in these old buildings are selling schlock (if I see one more floppy-eared stuffed bunny wearing a calico dress or one more wooden goose with a blue ribbon around its neck, I won't be responsible for what happens), but this irritating fact shouldn't detract from what may be our biggest victory: Thanks to preservationists, "commercial rehab" is no longer just a synonym for aluminum siding.

There was a time — not too long ago, either — when most developers seemed to believe the only good building is a new building, and the only good old building is one that's gone. In those days a walk down any street was sure to take you past at least one fenced-off site where a sound old structure was being demolished. That doesn't happen so much anymore. Older buildings still get flattened, to be sure, but not automatically. Nowadays developers who find themselves with an old building on their hands are likely to see it as an opportunity instead of a nuisance.

The concept of adaptive use — a concept we popularized — has entered the urban-design mainstream. I know we haven't won over everybody, and some old buildings survive by default merely because preservation laws — laws we fought for — make demolition difficult. That's fine with me. At least the buildings get saved, and if that's not winning, what is?

Maybe it's too soon to order cases of celebratory champagne, but surely we've earned at least a beer and a pretzel. So here's what we'll do: We'll find a historic district with crowded sidewalks lined with shops doing a roaring business in handsomely renovated old buildings. (We won't have to look far — they're everywhere.) We'll go into some lively watering-hole with buffed-up woodwork and buzzing cash registers. (Ditto.) We'll talk about what's still left to do. Mostly, however, we'll look around and allow ourselves to savor the simple, long-overdue, well-earned luxury of feeling good about how much we've already done.

Predisposed Against Disposal

Is there such a thing as a born preservationist? I intend the question in the most literal sense: Do some people come into the world with a "preservation gene" that predisposes them to a lifetime of saving things?

Heavy questions for a spring day. Here's what prompted them: A friend told me about an experience he had recently, one of those epiphanies that occurs when you least expect it. He was fumbling around with some insignificant thing — a shard of soap or a plastic grocery bag or something like that — and he found himself unable to part with it. He kept thinking that there was plenty of use left in it, that he might need it someday. I mean, this thing practically had "trash" written all over it, but he just couldn't throw it away.

With a shock, he realized that his actions were being controlled by something that ran deep in his blood. He knew that he literally had no choice but to save this thing. He hurriedly stuck it in a drawer, where it nested comfortably with 174 other items that he hadn't been able to dispose of in recent weeks.

Now I ask you, was this:

(a) a simple case of obsessive-compulsive behavior;

(b) yet another insidious effect of El Nino; or

(c) a clear-cut manifestation of genetically based preservationism?

The correct answer is (c). I'm sure of it, because I can pinpoint the similar episode that led me to recognize the workings of the preservation gene in my own psyche. It started with a sock.

In London many years ago I bought — for reasons that escape me now — a pair of socks emblazoned with brightly colored Union Jacks. Churlish friends referred to them as "Cornwallis's Revenge," but I wore them proudly until, in the way of socks since time immemorial, one of them disappeared. I agonized over the fate of the solitary remaining sock as if it were the last remnant of a rare and beautiful species of wildlife. Merely discarding it seemed out of the question, so I tried to justify my inclination to save it. Ignoring the fact that I have a deep-seated aversion to sock puppets and already possess a lifetime supply of dust cloths, I told myself that I was sure to find a use for the sock someday. And even if I don't, I reasoned, I certainly want to remember that trip to London, and what better *aide-memoire* than an orphaned piece of garish hosiery? (As you can see, I had blundered onto the slippery slope of preservation psychosis by this time.) I finally threw it away — a momentous act of will — but for hours afterward I felt a twinge of guilt every time I walked past the trash can.

As I reflect upon episodes such as this, it is increasingly obvious to me that I didn't *choose* to become a preservationist. It was preordained. I was genetically programmed that way, and fighting my natural inclinations would have been futile and self-destructive. Fortunately I recognized my preservationist proclivities fairly early on and embraced them.

Don't give me that condescending smirk: The mere fact that you're reading this book hints that you possess the gene too. Celebrate it. Come out, come out, whoever you are.

Even after finding peace with your...hmmm, let's call it your "condition," you'll find there are many questions still to be answered.

For instance, how can some people fritter away their time saving bits of string and wrinkled fragments of Christmas wrapping paper, yet never give a thought to saving an old building? Are they merely adept at suppressing their preservationist impulses, or is there a packrat chromosome unrelated to the preservation gene?

Is it possible to recruit converts to preservation, or must you be born to it? Can you acquire the preservation impulse late in life, or is it more likely that the tendencies were there — perhaps deeply suppressed — all along?

And what about cloning? — a scary prospect, admittedly, but think of the potential for rapidly swelling our ranks!

Eventually someone is sure to write a textbook on *psychologia preservationalis* (it will be fascinating reading, I expect, but probably not suitable for the kiddies), and then we'll gain a better understanding of what makes us tick. Until then, we can only watch for signs of the gene in ourselves, our friends and offspring — and rejoice when the signs appear.

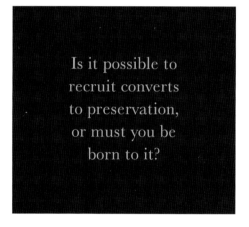

Is it possible to recruit converts to preservation, or must you be born to it?

The One and Only Barbara

While I'm in Miami this month for the National Preservation Conference, I have a little chore to perform.

I plan to drive over to the Art Deco District in Miami Beach and park somewhere on Ocean Drive. It will be early evening, when the lights are just beginning to come on, the beach is emptying out, and the bars and cafes are filling up.

I'm going to stroll up the street, along that incomparable blocks-long row of hotels. I'll watch the people having fun. I'll hear the music and the cash registers buzzing. I'll notice the new neon signs and the fresh paint jobs and the lines of cars looking for parking spaces. And somewhere I'm going to stop in the middle of the sidewalk and shout, "BARBARA CAPITMAN WAS RIGHT."

Some people thought Barbara was loony. Others were merely bemused, perceiving her as a latter-day female Don Quixote, while a few were known to become practically apoplectic at the mention of her name. She was unique. And more than any other single individual, Barbara Capitman was responsible for the remarkable renaissance that has transformed this part of Miami Beach during the past decade.

How did she do it? She nagged.

She was forever on the phone or buttonholing people in hallways and offices, usually carrying an armload of books and not caring that she looked as if she'd slept in her clothes. "They're going to tear down another hotel," she'd say in that inimitable voice. "Can't you help us?" You knew that she'd keep at you until you agreed. You did things for Barbara just to get her off your back, but it was never enough. She always wanted more.

She had this vision, you see. When she moved to Florida in the mid-1970s, there was no Art Deco District. There was just South Miami Beach, and it was a quiet, shabby place. But when Barbara looked at the streamlined shapes of those hotels, the terrazzo floors, the porthole windows and jazzy pylons, she saw things no one else did. She saw *Color!* and *Life!* and *The Future!* and couldn't understand why others saw only cracked stucco and peeling paint.

Gathering a cadre of creative people around her, she founded the Miami Design Preservation League and started her crusade. She won some terrific victories, most notably the listing of the Art Deco District in the National Register of Historic Places. There were losses, too: The demolition of the New Yorker Hotel in 1981 hit Barbara like a death in the family.

Through it all, she kept fighting — and nagging. She was an irresistible force, a whirlwind, the proverbial little old lady in tennis shoes, whose quavering voice and shy smile masked a steel-spined aversion to compromise.

Things finally began to fall into place. Barbara's Art Deco Society of America sprouted local chapters from coast to coast. In her beloved Miami Beach, the annual Art Deco Weekend drew locals and tourists alike to gaze at wonders they somehow had never noticed before. Renovated hotels and cafes began to open — and just as Barbara had predicted, people came. In a trickle that became a flood, they flew in from all over the world to shoot fashion layouts and music videos, to sip drinks on the breeze-cooled terraces, to sleep in retro-Deco beds in rooms smelling of salt air and fresh paint, to bask in the pizzazz of a new Hot Spot.

When Barbara died two years ago (some claim that the demolition of the Senator Hotel finally broke her heart), one obituary called her the First Lady of Art Deco. She was totally vindicated. I bet she was still not satisfied.

She certainly deserves a monument. Lummus Park would be a nice site — beneath the palms, but close to the bustle and dazzle of Ocean Drive. A simple upright slab with an inscription in snazzy Moderne letters:

BARBARA BAER CAPITMAN
1920 — 1990
She could see it when we couldn't.
She drove us nuts.
She was right.

Taking Note

When it comes to noticing things — really noticing them, I mean — no one does it better than Julius Knipl. That's why he's one of my heroes. Preservationists, after all, need keen powers of observation.

Mr. Knipl is a dumpy little middle-aged guy in a hat and a baggy suit who sports the kind of thin mustache seen on shady characters in 1940s movies. He always has a couple of camera bags slung around his neck because he makes his living as a real estate photographer. People hire him to take pictures of buildings they want to sell. I suspect he doesn't make much money at it, but he must be very good at his job. He certainly has a great eye for detail.

Julius Knipl, Real Estate Photographer is a comic strip that appears in a handful of weekly newspapers across the country. A couple of years ago several of the strips were collected in a book called *Cheap Novelties*. It's well worth seeking out — not only because artist Ben Katchor creates a dreamlike world unlike any other on the comics page, but also because Mr. Knipl's rambles constitute an instructive guide to the pleasures of noticing the quirky minutiae of the urban landscape that most people overlook.

Nothing escapes him. The sight of a distinctive signature on an inspection certificate leads my hero to muse that elevator inspectors "deserve to have their names publicly displayed in a suitable, transparent-faced frame" because they must "peer into the dismal void [that] lies at the heart of most buildings." Walking down the street, he hears "a feeble mechanical clang, followed by a blast of steam from an upper-story window." He wonders what could have made the noise, considers that it could have been anything from a shoe-tree maker to a rebuilder of milk-shake mixers to a good-luck-charm manufacturer, and finally walks on, having been "for a moment…reassured that light manufacturing still thrives in this city."

Mr. Knipl is not above an occasional flight of fancy: Consider, for instance, his rumination on the merits of installing public mustard fountains as a means of providing "every citizen in need with a schmeer of mustard" while simultaneously "improving a bland section of town." I suspect he's a closet preservationist, too. Investigating the space above the dropped ceiling of his office, he pokes his head into a world "where the heat of bygone summers rose to be churned by a fan, where a distinctive molding caught the attention of a now long-dead eye, and where luminous glass bowls hung in a turn-of-the-century night."

Mostly, though, Mr. Knipl is a matter-of-fact observer, a mental chronicler of the changing scene. Recalling a time when apartment buildings had names, he notes that they are now identified only by "bright numeric decals to which each tenant…is free to attach some personal significance." Coming upon a patch of newly-laid sidewalk, he knows that "through the grating of shoe leather, weather, and human accidents, and the appearance of those mysterious black spots," the white cement eventually will begin to blend with the older pavement, but (is there a hint of sadness here?) "because of the composition of new concrete, it will never sparkle at night."

One day, gazing up at an older building, Mr. Knipl realizes that there are hand-painted signs on "windows up as high as the twentieth floor." Pondering this curious and seemingly futile form of advertising, he wonders, "Could it be that people once had more acute eyesight?"

Maybe so. Maybe visual acuity, like a prehensile tail or the ability to amuse ourselves without electronic assistance, is something we've lost with the passage of time. Or maybe — and this seems more likely — we just need to cultivate the willingness to see. It can be a rewarding experience.

In New Orleans one day, I saw that someone had scrawled "my darlin Noo Awlins" in the wet cement of the sidewalk, perhaps years earlier. I had seen plenty of sidewalk love notes before, but they were all of the "John Loves Mary" variety. The idea that someone would call a city "darlin" delighted me.

When I showed the inscription to a friend who lived nearby, he said, "I never noticed that before." Julius Knipl certainly would have.

UPDATE: Readers unable to keep up with the musings of the inimitable Mr. Knipl in their local newspaper can find him — along with other samples of Ben Katchor's work — on the internet, at www.katchor.com.

Founding Mother

In contemporary photographs and portraits, she looks — there's no other word for it — sweet, like a middle-aged Melanie in a real-life *Gone with the Wind*. She was small and frail (a girlhood riding accident permanently injured her spine), but her physical infirmities masked a firm determination. If she hadn't been tough, she couldn't have become the mother of the American preservation movement.

Ann Pamela Cunningham stepped to the forefront of preservation history in December of 1853, when a Charleston, S.C., newspaper printed an article she had written decrying the sorry condition of George Washington's home, Mount Vernon. Years of neglect had left the estate a near ruin, its grounds overgrown, its noble piazza propped up with crude timbers; moreover, speculators were reportedly eyeing it as a prime development site. Addressing her appeal "To the Ladies of the South," Miss Cunningham urged them "to secure and retain the home and grave as a sacred spot for all coming time."

It was a staggering challenge. Remember this was the 1850s, when the United States was breaking apart over the issues of slavery and states' rights. Members of Congress were coming to blows, churches were splitting into northern and southern branches, longstanding relationships among friends and families were dissolving in bitterness. In this storm-wracked soil, Miss Cunningham's emotional appeal took root.

When her article was widely reprinted, committees of supporters sprang up on both sides of the Mason-Dixon Line. An organization — the Mount Vernon Ladies' Association — was chartered, and America's first nationwide preservation campaign was launched. Refusing to be daunted by the widening chasm of sectionalism, Miss Cunningham and her ladies worked quietly and steadily toward their goal. Finally, on February 22, 1860 — George Washington's 128th birthday — they took triumphant possession of Mount Vernon. They've owned it ever since.

Miss Cunningham taught us much of what we know about how preservation works. Her example set the course of the movement for several decades, inspiring groups all over the country to restore the homes of the Founding Fathers as shrines where citizens could refresh and reinvigorate themselves at the wellsprings of patriotism. She showed preservationists how to build a grassroots organization. She pioneered the celebrity fundraiser: Famed orator Edward Everett raised thousands of dollars for the campaign with a rousing two-hour speech on Washington that he delivered 139 times. Perhaps most important, she taught us that saving the nation's heritage transcends politics, that preservation can be a healing force, a standard around which all sorts of people can rally. It's a lesson we've forgotten and relearned many times in the past century.

At her retirement in 1874 Miss Cunningham wrote, "Ladies, the home of Washington is in your charge…. Let no irreverent hand change it; no vandal hand desecrate it with fingers of — *progress*!… Let one spot in this grand country of ours be saved from *change*!" Despite her plea, Mount Vernon has changed in many ways. Gardens and outbuildings have been reconstructed. Interiors have been repainted and refurnished numerous times, reflecting advances in the pursuit of historical accuracy. Interpretive programs have been revised to present a truer, but still evolving, picture of the past. More than a century after its incredible rescue, Mount Vernon is America's second most famous house, a place of pilgrimage, an icon — but still (and probably forever) a work in progress.

I've never seen Miss Cunningham's grave, but I imagine she lies under a modest tombstone in her native South

Carolina. Her true monument, of course, stands on the banks of the Potomac. Now, at the height of the vacation season, tourists are swarming over the grounds, lining up to troop through the once-shabby rooms, photographing one another in front of the piazza that nearly collapsed.

Most of these visitors have never heard of Ann Pamela Cunningham, don't realize that she would have been 180 years old on August 15. They don't know — as we, her heirs, do — that in the process of saving something wonderful she created something even better.

UPDATE: In 2003, the National Building Museum mounted a handsome exhibit entitled "Saving Mount Vernon: The Birth of Preservation in America" to commemorate the 150th anniversary of Miss Cunningham's campaign. Forty-three years earlier, the National Trust honored the Mount Vernon Ladies' Association with its first-ever Crowninshield Award, the nation's most prestigious award for superlative achievement in preservation.

As for Miss Cunningham herself, several readers wrote to tell me that she is buried — under a modest monument, as I expected — in Columbia, S.C.

FRISKY BUILDINGS

If you ask me, the Walt Disney Company has a lot to answer for. First it scared us half to death with that wicked queen in *Snow White*. Then, just when we were about to put that trauma behind us, it killed off Bambi's mother, Old Yeller, and the Lion King's dad. And now, not content with having turned Pocahontas into a Native American Barbie doll, it's come up with a musical version of *The Hunchback of Notre Dame* starring a cuddly Quasimodo and a coterie of wacky, wisecracking gargoyles. Is there no end to the horror?

Now for the good news. While churning out movies by the dozen, Disney has also been putting up buildings right and left — not just ersatz fairy-tale castles but hotels and stores and office buildings, too, some of which are outright masterworks. It's all detailed by architecture critic Beth Dunlop in a lavishly illustrated book called *Building a Dream* (Abrams, 1996).

Dunlop reminds us that Disney's in-house designers (the "Imagineers") have steadily turned out excellent — and woefully underrated — work. Preservationists owe them a great debt for the meticulously crafted Main Street buildings at Disneyland and Walt Disney World, which have helped open visitors' eyes to the charm of turn-of-the-century American architecture. There's also

much to appreciate in the decidedly more off-kilter — but no less skillfully designed — version of Main Street on view at Disneyland's Toontown, where the cartoonish buildings bulge and sag in all directions and the lettering on the "Planning Commission" sign doesn't quite fit.

Disney architecture really came into its own with the arrival of Michael Eisner as CEO in the mid-1980s. Having cemented a corporate commitment to top-quality, unconventional design, Eisner has commissioned world-famous architects to turn giddy visions into concrete reality. Michael Graves's Team Disney Building in Burbank is one of many wonderful buildings that have resulted. It's a temple fit for a modern-day Acropolis — but in place of languid, chiton-draped caryatids, Graves gives us Sleepy, Dopey, Grumpy, and the rest of the gang, all perched under the pediment and working mighty hard to hold up the roof.

Admittedly, these buildings aren't to everyone's taste: One critic has called them "architorture." But I happen to think they're terrific — *important*, even. Here's why.

They make me smile. When was the last time a building did that for you? Someone — I forget whether it was Vitruvius or Groucho Marx — once said that architecture should exhibit "commodity, firmness and delight." If you believe, as I do, that "delight" generally gets pretty short shrift, a structure like Robert A. M. Stern's Feature Animation Building in Burbank is a breath of fresh air. Sporting roof shapes that echo headgear worn by the Mad Hatter in *Alice in Wonderland* and Mickey Mouse in the "Sorcerer's Apprentice" segment of *Fantasia*, Stern's building fairly shouts, "Hey, lighten up, everybody, this stuff is supposed to be fun!"

These buildings demand attention. Architecture is supposed to be frozen music, but much of what's been built in recent decades is more like frozen Muzak — mere background noise, not even meant to be noticed, neither attractive enough nor ugly enough to merit a second glance. This is a dangerous state of affairs. Perhaps the most important thing about the Disney buildings is that they make idiotic noises, hit you in the face with a pie, and force you to notice them.

Like it or not, it's impossible to ignore Graves's over-the-top Dolphin Hotel at Disney World, its bold geometry decked out in turquoise and coral and topped with a brace of dolphins the size of Godzilla. It's the ideal antidote to the insidious, boredom-induced form of architectural blindness that makes us stop caring about buildings altogether, stop demanding that they be designed better, stop noticing when the good ones are threatened.

So, Disney, what's next? A laugh-a-minute *Beowulf* or a cheerily tuneful retelling of *Moby-Dick* we can do without. But buildings that make us smile, sit up, and pay attention — now there's something we need a lot more of. Stop spinning in your grave, Walt, and tell Eisner's architects to keep up the good work.

FOWLER'S FOLLIES

en die, but ideas live on — even when they're slightly screwy.

As proof of this maxim, consider an ad for an octagonal house that recently ran in *Historic Preservation News*. The sales pitch stated that the house was built in 1860, but I could have guessed that. Most of this country's octagonal houses — and there are more of them than you might think — were built in the decade immediately preceding the Civil War. And most of them are the legacy of one man: Orson Squire Fowler.

Contemporary images of Fowler show one of those great 19th-century faces full of boundless confidence and bright-eyed grit. His is the face of a man who believes he can find a better way of doing everything.

Fowler first achieved fame as a phrenologist, running his hands over thousands of skulls and teaching eager clients how to "exercise" various parts of their brains as a means of improving the character traits supposedly lodged therein. But he didn't stop there. Over the years he championed many causes, both noble and off-the-wall. He was a lifelong supporter of equality for women. He spoke out for children's rights and penal reform and was a pioneer in the fields of marriage counseling, sex education, and shorthand. He extolled the benefits of hydropathy and mesmerism, railed against the evils of tobacco and tight-laced corsets, and published the first edition of Walt Whitman's *Leaves of Grass*.

He took up architecture in 1848 with the publication of *A Home for All, or a New, Cheap, Convenient, and Superior Mode of Building*. "Why continue to build in the same SQUARE form of all past ages?" he asked. "Nature's forms are mostly SPHERICAL. Then why not apply her form to houses?" Since a spherical house would be a bit difficult to build, Fowler recommended the next best thing: an octagonal house, which he asserted would be both practical ("a given length of octagon wall will enclose one fifth more floor space than the same length of wall in a square shape") and attractive ("the more the angle approaches the circle, the more beautiful").

Applying his theory to practice, Fowler build his own octagon near Fishkill, N.Y. Utilizing a material he called the "gravel wall" (actually a concrete-like mixture of lime, sand, gravel, and water), he and a few laborers erected a house that stood three stories tall and featured a wide veranda encircling each floor and a many-windowed cupola atop the flat roof. Within were "sixty rooms, but not one too many," including a bedroom and dressing room for each member of the family and plenty of closets in the odd spaces between the square rooms and the octagonal shell.

Neighbors called the house "Fowler's Folly," but Fowler loftily ignored them. "No labor of my life has given me more lively delight than the planning and building of my own house," he wrote, urging others to follow his example. And plenty of people did just that: More than a thousand octagonal houses were erected during the 1850s, most of them inspired by *A Home for All*, which went through at least nine printings.

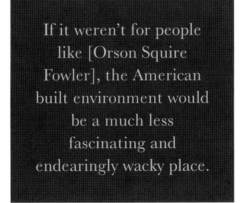

If it weren't for people like [Orson Squire Fowler], the American built environment would be a much less fascinating and endearingly wacky place.

Hard times eventually forced Fowler to allow his own octagon to be turned into a boarding house. Then, after several of the boarders were stricken with typhoid (probably caused by cesspool seepage through those much-vaunted gravel walls), Fowler sold the place. It sank into ruin and was demolished in 1897.

As for Fowler himself, he was neither the first nor the last celebrity to be brought low by a sex scandal. He raised eyebrows with his 1870 book *Creative and Sexual Science*, a 1,052-page tome intended to teach married couples "how to love scientifically." Raging against contemporary social mores, he urged women to find "summun bonum enjoyment" in sex — and landed in big trouble. A colleague charged him with delivering "private lectures to ladies…of an immoral character, and often grossly obscene in action and speech." The *Chicago Tribune* called him a "bird of prey" in a story headlined "Under the Cloak of Science He Disseminates the Seeds of Vice." His reputation shattered, Fowler died in obscurity in 1887.

But his ideas live on in the octagonal houses that dot the landscape from California to New England. Next time you stumble on one of them, think kind thoughts about Orson Squire Fowler. If it weren't for people like him, the American built environment would be a much less fascinating and endearingly wacky place.

PUPPETRY IN MOTION

There's a great master's thesis waiting to be written on *The Role of Puppet Shows in the 20th-Century History of the American Preservation Movement*. It'll be brief but pithy, and it'll be set in San Antonio, Tex.

Think "San Antonio" and two things come to mind: the Alamo and the River Walk. I'm not going to say any more about the former because, as a native Texan, I'm not expected to think rationally about the Alamo. But a recent visit to San Antonio has set me to thinking a lot about the River Walk — especially about how it almost didn't get built.

The San Antonio River lazes through the center of the city in a big horseshoe loop. Looking at it today, narrow and jade-green and docile, it's hard to imagine that this pussycat of a river was once a tiger. But it was: Floods were a frequent occurrence, and after a particularly violent one in 1921 caused $50 million in damage and left 50 people dead, the city fathers thought about channeling the river into big pipes and paving it over. Most downtown businessmen were all for it, but a group of local women thought it was a terrible idea.

The women were the San Antonio Conservation Society, founded in 1924, and the river wasn't the only thing they were concerned about. The city's historic Market House, an 1859 Greek Revival gem, was threatened with demolition, and landmarks such as the Spanish-era missions and the Governor's Palace were falling into ruin. Fearing that San Antonio's soul was being destroyed, the ladies decided to do something about it. Emily Edwards, who had been a drama teacher and stage designer before becoming president of the society, came up with the idea of a puppet show.

In September 1924, the ladies presented their show, *The Goose with the Golden Eggs*, to the city commissioners. The cloth hand-puppets included lifelike representations of the five commissioners, a stage manager, Mr. and Mrs. San Antonio, and a goose whose eggs symbolized the city's unique characteristics. The script, written in rhyme, depicted an argument between Mr. San Antonio (complaining that old buildings and narrow streets were impediments to progress) and his wife (urging the preservation of the city's heritage). At the final curtain the stage manager exhorted the commissioners to "save Old San Antonio — ere she die!" and the goose took a bow.

I'd love to tell you that the commissioners were immediately won over and everyone lived happily ever after, but that didn't happen. The Market House got demolished after all, and it was many years before the city finally adopted architect Robert Hugman's plans to create the River Walk that is now downtown San Antonio's glory. But the puppet show did plant a seed that has grown into a strong preservation ethic and a thriving tourism industry — and it also established the Conservation Society as a force to be reckoned with.

The society is still going strong, hip-deep (at this writing) in issues ranging from the threatened demolition of the historic Centro de Artes building to the proposed construction of a huge golf resort on environmentally sensitive land north of the city. It is a model organization, feisty and enormously savvy. When I asked a member why the Society's name employs the word "conservation" instead of "preservation," she said, "If we were the San Antonio Preservation Society, our nickname would be 'SAPS' — and we're definitely not." Good answer.

When I was in San Antonio I bought a poster of San Fernando Cathedral, parts of which date to the mid-18th century. It shows a night view of the cathedral, the details of its facade outlined in little white lights. In the shadow of the church, a fiesta is in full swing: People are eating tacos and cotton candy, and a Ferris wheel spins in a blur of bright neon. It's a scene right out of a preservationist's dream, a seamless blend of yesterday and today, reverence and revelry, in an environment that is richly textured, attractive, lively, and fun.

Every community ought to be like that. Maybe we need more puppet shows.

UPDATE: The history of preservation in San Antonio is exhaustively recounted in Lewis F. Fisher's *Saving San Antonio: The Precarious Preservation of a Heritage* (Texas Tech University Press, 1996). A rousing summary of the founding of the Conservation Society — including photos of the 1924 puppets — can be found on the SACS website, www.saconservation.org.

Castle in the Sand

Once there was a little girl who spent happy times with her father at the seashore, building sandcastles. When the waves washed them away, the little girl would cry, "Someday I want a castle that doesn't fall down."

One day the little girl's father went away on a quest. Many years later there came a message from a faraway land: Her father was dead, but he had left something for her. So she went to the faraway land, where she found that her father had built her the castle she had wished for. She settled in and (surely you could see this coming) lived happily ever after.

Pure fantasy, right? But it actually happened. Sort of. In Arizona.

You drive south from downtown Phoenix until the auto-repair shops and modest houses give way to rocky expanses of scrubby desert underbrush. Rugged mountains loom ahead, but just as the road begins to climb in earnest, you turn left. After awhile, a green wooden sign appears: MYSTERY CASTLE.

This castle doesn't resemble the images on the travel posters from Spain or Bavaria. It hunkers down into the rubbly landscape, and only the sharp-edged outlines of windows and roof keep it from looking like a random pile of rocks. When you park the car and walk closer, the exuberant complexity of the place begins to reveal itself in a welter of jutting beams and balconies, glints of color and reflected light, a thicket of chimneys, and a pair of antennae (light standards? flagpoles?) straight out of Buck Rogers.

The Mystery Castle is Mary Lou Gulley's home, her burden, her joy.

When Mary Lou was a child in Seattle, her father left home one day and never came back. She believes now that he may have fled to Arizona in a panicky attempt to cure his tuberculosis, but back then she knew only that her daddy was gone.

Mary Lou and her mother gradually put their lives back together. Then in 1945, some 17 years after he disappeared, Boyce Gulley sent his daughter a letter from his deathbed. He told her a castle was waiting for her in Phoenix. He had built it with his own hands to his own design. It had 18 rooms on almost as many different levels. There were 13 fireplaces, an underground bar, and a stone doghouse shaped like a teepee.

The castle held secrets: Loose stones concealed, among other things, gold nuggets and $74 in nickels and dimes. A trapdoor revealed a strongbox that held a photograph of Boyce Gulley, letters addressed to Mary Lou, and a wallet containing two $500 bills.

Above all, the castle displays Boyce Gulley's skill and ingenuity as both an innovative artist and a dedicated scavenger. He purchased a carload of glass refrigerator dishes and made windows from them. Clinker bricks and decorative tiles embellish every wall, both inside and out. Beds are mounted on rails so they can be moved across the room or concealed in wall niches. Slabs of stone above a fireplace are arranged to suggest the Grand Canyon. What appears to be a broken Doric column turns out to be the trunk of a saguaro cactus cast in cement. Pebbles inlaid in floors assume the form of sinuous snakes.

Whatever Mary Lou felt when she saw the place for the first time, she eventually fell in love with it. She shows it off to approximately 70,000 visitors annually, and has seen it featured on television and in magazines ranging from *Life* to *Catholic Digest*. One room displays local crafts for sale, another has been turned into a one-of-a-kind chapel that hosts several weddings a year.

Is it great architecture? Maybe not, but who's to say?

Is it worth preserving? Absolutely. And that's what Mary Lou spends a lot of time thinking about these days.

What do you do with a castle? What's the future of a fantasy? A neighbor has offered to buy the place, but Mary Lou is reluctant to sell. The City of Phoenix might want to acquire it as a museum, but she isn't sure that's a good idea, either.

Still, as she ponders a somewhat uncertain future, Mary Lou Gulley remains serene. She knows the waves can never knock her castle down again. Phoenix is a long way from the sea.

Out in Front

In the midst of all the hoopla about the National Trust's 50th anniversary, I almost overlooked the addition of the Stonewall Inn to the National Register of Historic Places.

In case you don't recognize the name, the Stonewall Inn is a gay bar in New York's Greenwich Village. In the course of my ongoing and exhaustive research on the subject of Seedy Places Where History Was Made, I visited the Stonewall a couple of years ago. Let me tell you, the Ritz it ain't. Outside, it was nondescript at best. Inside, it was dim (a good thing, since it struck me as the sort of place that looks best in near-darkness) and dank, with the smell of many years' worth of cigarette smoke and spilled beer emanating from the walls and floor.

Clearly, the Stonewall didn't make it to the National Register on the basis of its architectural splendor. And while the building was originally constructed (as a pair of stables, incidentally) in the 1840s, antiquity isn't one of its strong points, either. What makes the Stonewall significant is what happened there in the early morning hours of June 28, 1969.

Police raided the bar that night, which was not an unusual occurrence in those days. But this time the Stonewall's patrons — some of them in drag — fought back, a turn of events that most definitely *was* unusual. The ensuing near-riot, which continued intermittently over the next several nights, is generally considered to have marked the birth of the Gay Pride movement and has been enshrined as a watershed event of such significance that chroniclers of gay and lesbian history routinely divide their narrative into "before Stonewall" and "after Stonewall" eras.

You may be surprised, as I was, to learn that the Stonewall Inn is the first property to be added to the National Register specifically because of its association with gay and lesbian history. This official recognition of the site of an important turning point in our cultural history offers a welcome opportunity to acknowledge the enormous contribution that gays and lesbians have made to the cause of preservation in America.

It isn't exactly news, though we've treated it as if it were a secret best left undiscussed, that gays have traditionally been in the vanguard of efforts to revitalize historic neighborhoods. In city after city, as any savvy observer of the urban scene can tell you, the first sign that a shabby block might be on the brink of rebirth was the appearance of new residents driving cars (or, more recently, SUVs) with pink-triangle or rainbow-flag bumper stickers. And if you go on many historic-district house tours, chances are you're no longer surprised to find out that the beautiful Victorian rowhouse you've been admiring was restored by a same-sex couple.

(Question: Could it be that gay men and women have an intrinsic preference for older neighborhoods, just as they have a gift for biting wit, an ear for show tunes, and a knack for knockout window treatments? Now, there's an intriguing subject for a master's thesis if I ever heard one.)

It comes down to this: Preservationists have been loud — and rightly so — in our praise of the urban pioneers who have turned so many neighborhoods around, but we've been skittish about acknowledging that much of that hardy pioneer stock is gay. Happily, this don't-talk-about-them-and-maybe-they'll-go-back-to-being-invisible attitude is fad-

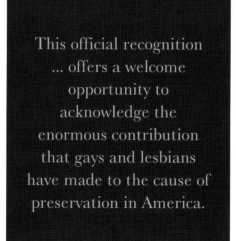

This official recognition ... offers a welcome opportunity to acknowledge the enormous contribution that gays and lesbians have made to the cause of preservation in America.

ing. The program for the 1999 National Preservation Conference included a field session that examined the role of the gay community in revitalizing some Washington, D.C., neighborhoods, and an evening reception gave "gays, lesbians and friends in preservation" a chance to socialize. (At a similar gathering two years ago in Santa Fe, I overheard one of my all-time favorite snippets of conversation: "What a nice surprise to see you here! I had no idea you were...um...a preservationist.")

For as long as I can remember, there's been a lot of talk about welcoming members of minority communities to the preservation movement, and we all know that self-conscious efforts to be "welcoming" are often painfully awkward. Well, in this case, everyone can relax. In a very real sense, gays and lesbians don't need to be welcomed. We've been here all along — often out in front, waiting for everyone else to catch up.

TWIN PEAKS

Don't ever think you've heard it all, because you haven't. As a case in point, I want to tell you about a man named Elton Pearson and what he and his friends have been up to in Toluca, Ill.

Toluca is about 40 miles northeast of Peoria. That's coal-mining country — or at least it used to be. In the early years of the 20th century, when the mines were going full blast, Toluca was a thriving place. But in the 1920s the mines closed and the population shrank (it's down to about 1,400 these days), and Toluca settled into its new role as a quiet town that had been shouldered aside by time and the fickle goddess called Progress.

Toluca does have a tangible reminder of its glory days, however: two giant piles of shale on the southern edge of town. This part of Illinois is pretty flat, so these 200-foot-tall slag heaps, as they're known locally, are a major landscape feature — not exactly the Alps, of course, but sufficiently prominent that the town is sometimes called Slag City. Townspeople have given the mini-mountains an affectionate nickname: the Jumbos. They're depicted, with varying degrees of verisimilitude, on the city's official stationery, on the masthead of the *Toluca Star Herald*, on the signs that welcome visitors to town. People will tell you that Toluca has three claims to fame: Mona's and Capponi's, two Italian eateries that have a large and enthusiastic regional clientele, and the Jumbos.

In the mid-1990s, they started disappearing. Contractors were hauling away the slag for use as fill. Someone said the Toluca Jumbos were in danger of becoming the Toluca Molehills. That's when Elton Pearson, a retired electrician, stepped in. Seeing the slag heaps as a monument to the town's industrial heritage and dreaming of the day when they might be developed as a recreational site, Pearson stationed himself on the sidewalk outside the post office and asked people to sign a petition protesting the gradual destruction of the Jumbos. He collected 226 signatures in three hours.

The city responded to this groundswell by buying the Jumbos and 101 acres surrounding them, and everyone breathed easier for a while. But one day a city road crew gouged a big chunk out of one of the Jumbos to build a road to a new sewage treatment pond. So Pearson and others cranked up the "Save the Jumbos" campaign again — and this time the city, with strong support from the mayor, did the right thing. On October 14, 1996, in addition to deciding to sell a 1972

Chevrolet dump truck and setting Halloween "trick or treat" hours from 5 to 8 p.m., the city council adopted a resolution declaring the Jumbos "part of the heritage of the City of Toluca, to be preserved and protected."

The "Save the Jumbos" campaign got a lot of press coverage (you can guess what the headlines said: "Heaps of History in Toluca," "Toluca Is Heaping with Pride," that sort of thing) and Elton Pearson was usually cast in the role of crusading hero. Last year he stepped down from the board of Toluca Coal Mine Preservation and Development, Inc., citing fears that he could "no longer be a help to our project" — but the effort he launched goes on. The organization has received some funding support from various sources, and work on stabilizing and enhancing the Jumbos got underway last spring.

Ditch the jargon, strip away the rhetoric, and preservation becomes simply a matter of deciding that something is worth hanging on to. Maybe it's an old barn or a big house with tall white columns or an ancient tree in the town square. Maybe it's a pair of slag heaps. Whatever it is, you realize that its disappearance would rob you of something important, so you decide to save it.

That's what people in Toluca decided, and as a result, they can look out their windows today and see a monument to their past — two monuments, in fact — looming against the sky just south of town. We should all be so lucky.

PERFECT WORLDS

Time is short, so make your reservations soon. This year's Donna Reed Festival is scheduled for June 12-19 in Denison, Iowa. Be there.

Donna grew up on a farm just outside of Denison. According to a festival press kit, she milked cows, drove the tractor, sewed her own 4-H uniform, and won a blue ribbon at the Iowa State Fair for a pan of biscuits. Back then, her name was Donnabelle Mullenger.

After high school, she went to California to study drama and business (she needed something to fall back on if the acting didn't work out) at Los Angeles City College. She entered some beauty contests, too, and when she was named Campus Queen and got her picture in the newspapers, her telephone started ringing. Donnabelle Mullenger signed a contract with MGM and became Donna Reed.

Though she appeared in 42 movies

and won an Academy Award for her performance in *From Here to Eternity*, she may be best remembered as Jimmy Stewart's loving wife in the classic *It's a Wonderful Life*. The model-wife-and-mother role suited her so well that she later played it for eight years on television's *The Donna Reed Show*.

I once found a TV channel that was broadcasting a Seven-Day Donnathon — a full week of non-stop *Donna Reed Show* reruns. It made for soothing viewing. In such a relentlessly wholesome, black-and-white world where nothing really bad ever happened, Donna was a cheerful helpmate to her husband, a wise counselor to her children, a consummate homemaker who twirled into her spotless kitchen and emerged moments later, every hair in place, bearing pot roasts and layer cakes. She was perfect. No wonder they're proud of her in Denison.

In addition to several educational workshops and an appearance by Shelley Fabares, who was Donna's TV daughter and is currently playing a live-in girlfriend on the sitcom *Coach* (a role of which I'm not sure Donna would approve, but never mind), the festival offers a preservation angle, too: Sponsors are raising funds to restore Denison's Ritz Theater. I'm really glad to hear that. They're not just saving a building. They're preserving a means of escape.

When I was growing up, I spent a lot of time at two theaters in Plainview, Tex.: the State and the Granada. The State was a small, plain theater where we yelled and threw popcorn and scuffled in the aisles during the westerns and comedies that filled the double-feature bill. A Saturday afternoon at the State was an experience in moviegoing as contact sport.

The Granada was different. Nowadays I'd call it a movie palace; back then, I just knew it was a vast and wonderful place where yelling was unthinkable. A ceiling studded with dim stars was suspended over walls that simulated a castle, with Spanish shawls draped over fake balconies and dripping fountains set into niches. (We learned to avoid those fountains. If we sat too near them, the sound of the water sent us on frequent trips to the restroom.) At the center of it all was a screen of truly monumental dimensions, thundering with the exploits of pirates, knights, Walt Disney characters, and atomic-mutant monsters on a rampage.

I distinctly remember more than one afternoon when I thought, sitting there in the plushly upholstered splendor of the Granada, "I wish the whole world was like this." A decade later, Donna Reed brought that sentiment into our living rooms. She created, inhabited and exemplified a world in which parents were strong and loving and relatively affluent, adolescents were polite and well-adjusted, prob-

> Escape is essential now and then, but it's hard to find it in a shoebox-sized theater with a name like Asphalt Gardens Shopping Plaza Multiplex Cinema 17.

lems were relatively minor, and endings were always happy. Watching, we knew it was ludicrously unreal, but we couldn't help wishing the whole world could be like that.

That's why I'm glad they're memorializing Donna Reed by restoring an old movie house. Escape is essential now and then, but it's hard to find it in a shoebox-sized theater with a name like Asphalt Gardens Shopping Plaza Multiplex Cinema 17. We need to save lots of Palaces and Rialtos and Majestics — and Granadas.

In fact, when the folks in Denison finish restoring their Ritz, I wish they'd take on the Granada. I hear it's been subdivided into two smaller theaters. I'll bet the fountains are dry, and I'm worried that they've turned off the stars, too.

Donna wouldn't like that.

UPDATE: Having suffered a number of indignities in recent years, the Granada closed its doors in 1997. The building still stands, a vacant but imposing landmark on Plainview's Broadway. Just down the street, the smaller and less opulent Fair Theatre has been restored; it reopened in 1999 as a venue for live performances and meetings. The kid-battered State, on the other hand, long ago followed ten-cent popcorn and Saturday afternoon double-feature westerns into oblivion. I'm not sure what sort of building now occupies the site, though it occurs to me that the presence of a foot-thick layer of discarded Milk Duds and bubble gum might have rendered any redevelopment infeasible.

Meanwhile, the Donna Reed Festival is still doing boffo business in Denison. The renovated Ritz reopened in 1995 and is now known as the Donna Reed Center for the Performing Arts. Information on the theater and festival can be found at www.donnareed.org.

Speaking of Donna, a reader wrote to remind me that not all of her screen roles were of the apple-pie-and-gingham-apron variety. In fact, she won her Oscar for playing a prostitute in *From Here to Eternity*. Snuggling up against her in one scene, boyfriend Montgomery Clift says, "Gee, this is just like being married, isn't it?"

Shooting him a Meaningful Look, Donna replies, "It's better."

Further evidence — if any were needed — that when it came to creating a perfect world, nobody out-did Donna.

Looking Injustice in the Face

What should a monument to injustice look like? Should it be tall, threatening and sharp-edged, gleaming black and blood-red? Or should it be smaller, more slithery, a poisonous menace half-hidden among rocks and shadowy vines?

Or might it take the form of an isolated valley dotted with scrubby bushes where clouds of wind-borne grit sometimes blot out the rugged mountains looming on all sides?

That's how Manzanar looks.

Located in Inyo County, Calif., east of Mount Whitney and west of Death Valley, Manzanar was the site of the first facility constructed by the U.S. government to house Japanese-American internees during World War II. These places — there were ten of them, scattered from California to Arkansas — were called "war relocation centers," yet "concentration camps" would be a more accurate label.

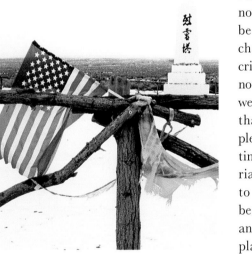

When President Roosevelt signed Executive Order 9066 a few weeks after Pearl Harbor, he set in motion a process that uprooted some 110,000 Japanese Americans from their homes on the West Coast. Most of them were U.S. citizens, either naturalized or native-born, and none of them had been formally charged with a crime. That did not matter. They were "Japs," and that label, coupled with racist-tinged war hysteria, was enough to justify their being rounded up and penned in at places such as Manzanar. For thousands of Japanese Americans now reaching middle age, "relocation" was the defining experience of childhood and adolescence.

Manzanar was recently designated a National Historic Site, open to the public under the auspices of the National Park Service. But there's a problem. You see, there isn't much left of the camp itself: a weathered auditorium, the foundations of the vanished wood-and-tarpaper barracks, remains of the cemetery and gardens, and a couple of stone guardhouses. Not much more. The Park Service has to figure out how to interpret a grim episode of American history at a place that's hardly there.

A team of landscape architects — all of Japanese descent, all former internees — has offered advice on site design, emphasizing the importance of the landscape itself as a powerful element in Manzanar's story. Park Service experts in inter-

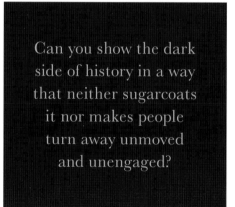

Can you show the dark side of history in a way that neither sugarcoats it nor makes people turn away unmoved and unengaged?

pretation are drawing up a general management plan that may propose the installation of an interpretive exhibit in the auditorium and possibly the reconstruction of a building or two. But there's really a much bigger issue here.

What it boils down to is this: How do you encourage visitors to stare into the ugly face of hate and prejudice? Can you show the dark side of history in a way that neither sugarcoats it nor

makes people turn away unmoved and unengaged? Is it possible to make people think about the unthinkable?

Several sites around the country have wrestled with these questions recently — and have come up with some remarkably good answers. At Kelly Ingram Park in Birmingham, Ala., a series of sculptures depicts the violence of the civil-rights struggles in a presentation that is both confrontational and poetic. In Salem, Mass., an award-winning memorial to 20 victims of the 1692 witch trials uses subtle symbolism to evoke the tragedy eloquently, even across a span of three centuries. And here in Washington, D.C., the United States Holocaust Memorial Museum thrusts thousands of visitors daily into a gut-wrenching, no-holds-barred encounter with genocide of chillingly recent vintage.

Any of these might offer an instructive model for meaningful interpretation at Manzanar. But there's still another possible approach. A character in J.D. Salinger's *Raise High the Roof Beam, Carpenters*, speaking of Lincoln's Gettysburg Address, remarks that "51,112 men were casualties at Gettysburg, and if someone had to speak at the anniversary of the event, he should simply have come forward and shaken his fist at the audience and then walked off...." That sort of minimalism would be appropriate for Manzanar. Visitors, as they wander the dusty paths past the foundations of the barracks and pause to look at the "Soul Consoling Tower," could wear headphones that play two sounds: a solemn voice repeating the word "remember," and the Zen-like swish of a fist being shaken.

That should be enough to remind us that a monument to injustice might look like a mirror.

UPDATE: This piece generated lots of mail. A few readers wrote that my sympathy for the internees (who had constituted a genuine threat to national security and therefore deserved to be locked up) was an insult to the memory of the brave men who fought in World War II — while others noted that the U.S. Army's 442nd Regimental Combat Team, made up entirely of Japanese Americans, was one of the war's most highly-decorated units. Most interesting were the letters that included ideas for a memorial at Manzanar; Ms. Rosenberg's fifth-grade class at Bowman School in Lexington, Mass., had some especially good ideas.

At Manzanar itself, several structures have been rehabbed or reconstructed, and the auditorium is being restored for use as an interpretive center. An original mess hall, moved to a nearby community after the war, is being returned to Manzanar as part of an effort to give visitors a better idea of what camp life was like. Additional information, including a virtual tour, is available at the park's website, www.nps.gov/manz.

Here in Washington, D.C., a memorial to Japanese-American internees was recently completed a few blocks from the Capitol. It's a pretty, contemplative place. The names of the camps are inscribed on stone walls, and there's a shallow pool dotted with boulders and a big metal gong that is sounded on ceremonial occasions. At the center of it all is a soaring sculpture: a pair of gilded cranes entangled in barbed wire.

THE GREAT PRESERVATION NOVEL

Several years ago a bunch of us sitting around a dinner table came up with a scenario for a preservation operetta. Among other delights, it was to feature a chorus of construction workers wearing hard hats, t-shirts, and mirrored sunglasses who would swagger onto the stage and sing:

You say you got bad plaster?
Well, this ain't no crock
We got what you need
You need sssssshhhhheetrock.

At the climax of the operetta, all problems were to be solved by a sort of Old-House Fairy, who would hover above the stage, waving a wand and wearing a gauzy gown and a tool belt. One member of our group was certain that this was the role she had been born to play. "My hair will be long and golden," she rhapsodized, "and my feet will twinkle." I wasn't sure what that last part meant, but she was very insistent about it.

Like many other sure-fire smash-hit ideas, this one never came to fruition. I mention it now because of something that bothers me: Here we are, well into the last decade of the century, and no one has yet written the Great Preservation Novel.

At least two authors have taken a crack at it, however. One of them is English, the other American. Both books are funny, though only one of them intentionally so. Either would be a good read while sitting through a historic district commission meeting — or while lying down in front of a bulldozer.

The first is Tom Sharpe's *Blott on the Landscape*, which is best described with a word I don't use very often: rollicking. Published in the U.S. in 1984 by Vintage Books, *Blott* mines the comic vein of such British TV offerings as *Fawlty Towers* and *Are You Being Served?* to tell of Lady Maud Lynchwood's efforts to save her ancestral home from a superhighway. Lady Maud — who, like her house, is hulking, ungraceful, and asymmetrical — is pitted against bumbling planning officials and a husband who resolutely refuses to help produce an heir. Her ultimate triumph is wonderful, and so is this book. In fact, my only complaint is that it's too short.

The other contender is Edward LaGrande's *Saints in the Shadows*, also published in 1984 and set in New Orleans. Be forewarned: This is not great literature. It's a hoot.

Subtle characterization is not LaGrande's strong suit. The good guys — idealistic architect Will Strappet and curvaceous Felice Toussaint, director of the French Quarter Commission — are very good indeed. Relentless comic relief is provided by Boudin Johnson, who plays Sancho Panza to

Will's Don Quixote. Boudin is a Cajun. In fact, he is mega-Cajun. "How y'all are?" he is wont to bellow. "I sure am glad for you to met me, I mean to told you! Boo-danh, that's my front-name, and Jaw-sawn, that's my behind-name, too!" He also hollers "WHOOOOO-EEE!" a lot. You get the picture.

The bad guys are a thoroughly vile bunch. Vilest among them is Joe Cantrell, an unscrupulous developer whose nefarious schemes are abetted by a *femme fatale* named — you'd better sit down for this — Hart Talon. But the real villain of *Saints in the Shadows* is [ominous chord] modern architecture. Prince Charles would love this book. A cluster of sky-scrapers is described as "trim and hard as tombstones. Some were dizzying mirrors; others seemed black-marble mausoleums; still others scowled like concrete giants, their skins rough as beasts." One tower "appeared to house a blind and alien thing crouched inside, waiting. Its air-conditioners panted."

When Cantrell tries to build one of these behemoths in the French Quarter, the gumbo hits the fan. The ensuing mess involves corrupt officials, blackmail, Cajun cuisine, long-suppressed secrets, faded beauty queens, Mardi Gras, insidious Arab oilmen, budding romance, and arson. Sort of like *War and Peace*, but with fewer pages and higher humidity.

I'm beginning to think that the Great Preservation Novel won't be written in my lifetime, but I'm not too despondent. For now, *Blott on the Landscape* is terrifically entertaining, and *Saints in the Shadows* does at least provide fodder for the perfect made-for-TV movie.

Quick, somebody find out if we can get Lesley Anne Warren and Efrem Zimbalist, Jr.! Lights, camera, histrionics!

> Here we are, well into the last decade of the century, and no one has yet written the Great Preservation Novel.

UPDATE: Ten years later, the Great Preservation Novel still hasn't appeared.

Blott on the Landscape was filmed by the BBC and is now available on video. *Saints in the Shadows* hasn't made it to the screen — which, depending on your point of view, is either a blessing or a great pity.

OF PAINT, CLAY, AND MARBLE

I've visited two favorite historic places recently. It's been a serendipitous pilgrimage of healing.

It started when I drove to western Massachusetts for a friend's wedding. Like most road trips since September 11, the journey was an intensely patriotic experience. Flags hung from overpasses and the sides of barns, blazed from bumper stickers and living-room windows, snapped in the wind from courthouse flagpoles and car antennae. Some were store-bought banners in silk and gold fringe; others were obviously, heart-tuggingly, homemade, with stripes that weren't quite straight and stars that staggered in unruly rows.

There were signs, too. One of them was a big piece of plywood propped against a fence in front of a farmhouse somewhere in upstate New York. The board was painted white, and big red letters spelled out GOD BLESS AMERICA. I sped past it in a flash, and now I can't put it out of my mind.

I don't know whether the sign-maker is a man or woman, but I find myself thinking of him/her as "that guy."

On September 11, when those horrifying images appeared on his TV screen, I imagine that guy felt the way you feel when someone you love is sick or hurt and you can't fix it — but you have to do *something*, so you busy yourself with a chore of some kind to keep from falling apart. So he went to the barn and hauled out that big sheet of plywood that he'd always known would come in handy someday. He painted it white and, without thinking much about which words to write, added the big red letters. And it was okay that the letters were sort of clumsy and the words sort of slanted downhill, because he wasn't creating Art, he was just getting something out of his system before it made him explode.

Here's what that guy's sign felt like to me: a rush of anguish, a deep well of love.

The next day — a brilliant Sunday, with the year's last leaves sifting silently to the ground under a flawless sky — I went to Chesterwood, the country home where sculptor Daniel Chester French spent summers from 1897 to 1931. In the Chesterwood studio stand several early versions of French's monumental statue of Abraham Lincoln, variants in which you can see the artist grappling with the challenge of capturing Lincoln's spirit in clay, shifting the position of a hand here, tilting the head a bit there. French must have known that this was the work that his whole career had been pointing to. I pictured him laboring away in his shirtsleeves, pausing now and then to step out onto the little porch to rest and draw fresh inspiration from the tranquil beauty of the view across the valley to Monument Mountain.

Here's what Chesterwood felt like: all-enveloping peace.

Back in Washington a few nights later, I went to the memorial where French's Lincoln sits in his glowing marble shrine. Only a few other visitors were there, all of them, like me, reduced to awed silence by the statue's brooding presence. I marveled at the long road of tragedy, triumph, and remembrance that began in a cabin in Kentucky and led finally to

this temple beside the Potomac. I thought about French creating his masterpiece and I thought of that guy painting his sign. Then I just sat on the steps and didn't think of anything for a long while, letting the view and the

mild night air and the spirit of the place bear me up, float me along.

Here's what the Lincoln Memorial felt like: utter serenity, enormous power.

I wished that guy were there with me. I wanted him to see French's vision of Lincoln, grief-wounded but strong. I wanted to show him the view down the Mall to the Capitol dome gleaming impossibly white in the distance. I wanted to tell him, "See, it's all still here. It endures. We'll get through this."

But maybe he doesn't need to hear me say it. Maybe he already knows. Maybe he knew as soon as he finished painting that sign.

ALL TOGETHER NOW

This is a story of gasoline, preservation, irony, and pancakes. It began 70 years ago this year, when the Standard Oil Company announced plans to build a gas station at the corner of Meeting and Chalmers Streets in Charleston, S.C.

Charleston Mayor Thomas P. Stoney didn't like the idea of a gas station at that particular location, right in the historic heart of his city. In fact, Mayor Stoney was increasingly convinced that the forces of progress and change — hateful words — were turning his cherished hometown into something alien and ugly. He decided to see if something could be done to keep Charleston's spectacular architectural heritage intact.

The chain of events set in motion by Mayor Stoney in 1929 culminated two years later in the enactment of America's first municipal preservation ordinance, establishing the Old and Historic Charleston District to protect "the qualities which preserve property values and attract tourists and residents alike...." The visionaries who drafted and administered this ordinance not only "saved" historic Charleston but also sparked the passage of similar laws in hundreds of other communities — including Miami Beach, where many of the buildings in the famed Art Deco historic district weren't even built when the Charleston ordinance was adopted.

As a piece of legislation without precedent, the Charleston ordinance is a big, important stone in the foundation of today's preservation movement. Most of that foundation was laid in the years between 1931 and 1966, when the National Historic Preservation Act was passed. And right in the middle of that time span — 18 years after the Charleston ordinance and 17 years before the Act — the National Trust was born.

For half a century the Trust has fought the good fight, and it's worth remembering that there was no national organization to do that kind of fighting before the Trust was founded. We haven't won every battle. Penn Station is gone, along with the City of Paris store in San Francisco, Jobbers Canyon in Omaha, and far too many other great places gone to dust. But we've won more than our share of victories, too — victories made visible not only in buildings saved, but also in Main Streets and residential neighborhoods reborn, grassroots organizations established, better preservation laws enacted and enforced, new generations of preservationists informed and inspired, a national movement shaped and strengthened.

Maybe the single biggest thing the Trust has accomplished in the past 50 years is this: Before 1949, preservationists worked in isolation in their local communities, sure that they were doing the right thing but less sure that they were going about it in the right way. The existence of the National Trust means that today, no matter how far out in the boondocks they're working, preservationists know that they're part of something big and growing, something with credibility and clout and a strong record of success behind it. They no longer have to feel — as the people who drafted the Charleston ordinance must have felt — that they've embarked on a voyage for which no maps exist.

I promised you some irony, and here it is. Despite the ordinance, that Standard Oil station got built, right where Mayor Stoney didn't want it. It turned out to be a pretty grand place to get gas. In an effort to "fit in" with its historic neighbors, the station incorporated architectural elements from a demolished mansion, including mellow old brick, segmental window pediments, and fluted Ionic columns. Eventually it became something of a landmark in its own right. When it finally closed down a few years ago it was purchased — here's the most delicious irony of all — by the Historic Charleston Foundation, which now operates its Frances Edmunds Preservation Center in the little building that caused such a big ruckus.

The whole hassle-to-happy-ending scenario reminds me of a line from my favorite 1970s television sitcom, *Mary Hartman, Mary Hartman*. Whenever things got crazy, poor Mary would smile desperately and say, "Don't worry. Everything will be all right, and then we'll go to the House of Pancakes."

Everything, more or less, *has* turned out all right. So consider yourself cordially invited to join me and about 270,000 close friends for a well-earned celebration. We'll meet at the House of Pancakes. We'll write "Happy Birthday, National Trust" in bold strokes of maple syrup.

No Way to Treat a President

No one ever claimed that the President Monroe was one of Washington's most impressive landmarks. A nice-looking turn-of-the-century apartment building with Classical Revival details and an interesting pedigree, that's all it was. But this modest building has been the focus of a preservation battle that has raged for four years now, with no end in sight.

When it was constructed in 1902, the President Monroe was a precedent-setter. Unlike earlier Washington apartment buildings, it made no attempt to mimic the appearance of a single-family residence. In other words, it looked like what it was. Largely because of its significance as a pioneering example of a conventional multi-unit apartment house, the President Monroe was named a local historic landmark in 1991.

Before the designation was finalized, the owner of the now vacant apartment building knocked down part of the facade and the entrance portico. He claimed that the action was necessary in the wake of an arson fire, but an unnamed city official told a reporter that the demolition — carried out without a permit — looked like an act of deliberate vandalism.

Soon neighbors were complaining that the battered building was a haven for vagrants and drug dealers. The owner of a nearby shoe shop said that the President Monroe's derelict condition was scaring away his customers. Every few days the structure got boarded up, but the barriers always came down again. There were more fires, too — more than a dozen in 1991 alone.

By this time the President Monroe looked as if it belonged in Sarajevo. In May 1992 the owner applied for a permit to tear it down, but the Historic Preservation Review Board ruled that the building was still salvageable and that total demolition was unwarranted. A month later another fire caused extensive damage to the facade. Armed with a permit to remove only certain damaged areas, the owner demolished four-story-tall porches, lopped off the roof and top floor, and smashed the entire front wall.

Then things happened fast. The President Monroe landed in the lap of the Mayor's Agent, who had the power to determine its ultimate fate. The D. C. Preservation League (DCPL), a local organization formerly — and more forthrightly — known as Don't Tear It Down, argued that the owner's actions had made the President Monroe a case study in demolition by neglect and that allowing him to raze the building would make a mockery of the preservation ordinance. The Mayor's Agent, sounding a bit regretful, issued a demolition permit anyway. Quick as a flash, DCPL filed an appeal. And finally, last August the Court of Appeals ruled in the League's favor, saying that the Mayor's Agent had exceeded his authority in granting the demolition permit. There was talk of requiring the owner to restore the President Monroe to its pre-demolition appearance.

But if you're holding your breath in anticipation of a happy ending, you can forget it. What's happened in the wake of this ruling is…absolutely nothing.

A few months ago, when the President Monroe was sold, DCPL Administrator Rich Busch called the new owner to make sure he was aware of the property's landmark status. "Have you seen the building?" the owner asked incredulously. "It's a wreck." When Busch reiterated the League's determination to see the court decision enforced, the owner hung up the phone.

So what, if anything, has been gained in this battle of claims and counterclaims, flames and crowbars, decisions made and overturned? Well, for one thing, the President Monroe still stands (some of it, at least), and maybe it will be restored someday. Miracles do happen. And the D.C. preservation law has been strengthened, a fact that is probably enough to confirm this as a fight that was worth fighting on principle alone, if for no other reason.

Still, it's difficult to read victory in the sad, graffiti-daubed shell of wood and masonry that gapes in a weed-grown lot at 423 Massachusetts Avenue. People in the neighborhood still worry about fire, about the rats that scurry in and out of the rubble, about the scary goings-on in the shadowy recesses of the building in the dead of night. You can hardly blame them for thinking: If this is preservation, who needs it?

The fundamental lesson to be learned from the saga of the President Monroe, it seems to me, is a confirmation of something most preservationists have known all along. Old buildings have lots of enemies — fire, water, time, and termites, to name a few — but there's no enemy worse than an owner who doesn't care.

UPDATE: The beat-up, bombed-out ruin of the President Monroe stood for several months after this piece was written. It looked so convincingly apocalyptic that at one point a movie crew "decorated" the facade-less shell with furniture, paint, and wallpaper and used it as the backdrop for some scenes in a space-invasion movie.

And then, one day, the building just wasn't there anymore. There's quite a bit of new construction underway in the neighborhood, but the site of the President Monroe is still a vacant lot.

POETIC JUSTICE

I realize that a Christmas card or New Year greetings would be more appropriate to the season, but this is going to be a valentine, sung to the tune of "America the Beautiful."

The piece of America I'm talking about is Polk County, N.C., which has a landscape as rumpled up and tumbled about as an insomniac's bedspread. In this setting of forested mountains and placid valleys, noisy rivers and lacy waterfalls, most man-made constructions — except for some handsome log cabins — don't merit much notice. But the county does have a signature building, a structure that most people agree is the most important landmark around. It's the county courthouse, sitting in the middle of a grassy square in the little town of Columbus.

Like many of its counterparts all over the United States, this courthouse is a vernacular rendition of the Greek Revival, a classical tune played on a country fiddle. For all its simplicity, the building is a genuine architectural event, presiding with great dignity over the scattering of stores and houses that surround it. Outside, it has fine redbrown brickwork and a square-pillared portico, all topped off with a perky cupola. Inside, high-ceilinged offices are awash with light from tall windows, and twin staircases spiral upward with a spare elegance that wouldn't be out of place in a Shaker meetinghouse.

Lawyers, judges, and assorted miscreants have been conducting their business here since 1859. Decades of heavy use — all those licenses issued, deeds filed, gavels banged, verdicts rendered — left their mark, and by the 1990s the building looked pretty shabby. Someone decided Something Should Be Done, and before long a restoration committee was formed. The county government appropriated $1 million, and citizens chipped in with more than $400,000 — no mean feat in a county with not many people, not many of them rich.

When the work was done, Alan Peoples, a county commissioner and longtime friend, invited me to speak at the rededication. So on a glorious autumn day we gathered on the courthouse lawn, and here's what happened: A young woman named Lili Gil sang "The Star-Spangled Banner" in the loveliest voice I've heard in a long time; members of the VFW presented flags to the families of courthouse supporters who had died before the project was completed; various speakers — including me — said various things; and through it all some 400 people looked up at that cupola against the bluest of blue skies and smiled all over themselves.

Okay, so I'm a sucker for this sort of thing. The fact is, it just about did me in.

I thought about James Taylor and Ada Louise Huxtable. The former because he once sang a melancholy love song to a small town that included these lines:

Used to be part of the heartland, awful proud and strong
But deep deep down, peaceful and serene.
When people used to talk about the country,
That's what they used to mean.

The latter because she once wrote (I'm paraphrasing here) that people and communities generally get the kind of buildings they deserve.

Back in the 1850s, community leaders decided that Polk County deserved a courthouse that would be a noble specimen of fine architecture, bricksand-mortar proof that civilization had come to stay in the wilderness. They decided, in short, that Polk County

deserved a courthouse that would testify to the good sense and foresight of its people. A century and a half later, today's county residents made the same decision.

They had other options. I've been to some counties that transact official business in factory-built metal buildings or double-wide house trailers, while others (you know who you are) have installed themselves in new buildings that have all the charm and character of a bus-station restroom. Polk County could have gone that way too, but its people decided they wanted something better.

By making that decision, today's Polk Countians — residents of the kind of proud and strong, peaceful and serene place that James Taylor sang about — have shown that their forefathers were right. They got exactly what they deserve, and so did their courthouse.

FEASTING ON KIZHI

If anyone offers you a trip to Kizhi, take it. Just throw some clothes in a suitcase and go. Admittedly, it's not an easy trip: You have to take two or three planes and then a boat — but even if you have to ask someone to pack you in a crate and mail you there, it's worth it.

Kizhi is an island in Lake Onega, in a region of Russia known as Karelia. Before I went there recently on a National Trust Study Tour, I'd never heard of it. Now that I've seen it, I'll never forget it. And I'm not alone in thinking it's a great place. The first three Russian sites inscribed in UNESCO's World Heritage List, which includes our planet's most precious cultural and natural properties, were the historic centers of Moscow and St. Petersburg — and Kizhi.

In summer, Kizhi floats in a world reduced to two colors: the blue of sky and water and the green of everything else. It's a bit like northern Maine or Michigan, a beautifully tranquil landscape that makes you want to sit under a tree and daydream. But what sets this place apart isn't scenery; it's buildings.

Near the southern end of the island stands a complex of three structures: a bell tower (built in 1862), the Church of the Intercession (1764), and the Church of the Transfiguration (1714). All three are built entirely of wood, but that plain fact doesn't begin to suggest their incredible visual impact. They are — how many adjectives am I allowed? — fantastic, stupendous, awe-inspiring, delightful. Looking at them, you want to smile, shout, burst into applause, dance.

The Church of the Transfiguration, built without nails, is the most impressive: an extraordinary pile of brown logs and silver aspen shingles, gables, and domes going up and up and up. Depending on your vantage point and the slant of the light, it looks like an explosion in a sawmill, like a fantastic splintery dessert concocted for some giant gourmand by a chef who'd had too much caffeine, like a wooden geyser frozen in mid-eruption, like nothing you've ever seen before.

My first reaction to these buildings was simple and immediate: *Wow*. Later I came to a somewhat more articulate realization: This is why I got involved in preservation in the first place.

We preservationists have become adept at developing rational justifications for our interest in saving old buildings. We can go on at length about the economic benefits of preservation, about the role of old buildings in community revitalization, and their psychological value as links with our own past. This kind of data lends essential credibility to preservation, certainly, but has our emphasis on it made us hesitant to admit that we like old buildings for reasons that have to do with our eyes as well as our wallets?

At Kizhi all the cultural/socioeconomic rationale falls away. Walking around the complex didn't tell me anything about my roots. Nobody's ever going to convert these buildings into affordable housing or a shopping mall, nor is their presence going to generate any spinoff rehab activity in the surrounding neighborhood. No matter. Like hundreds of others, the Kizhi buildings are worth saving simply because they are so wonderful to look at. It's a matter of [*WARNING: I'm about to use the "a"-word here*] aesthetics. There, I've said it and I'm glad.

Guidebooks make much of Kizhi's atmosphere of myth and magic. Dental problems, for instance, are said to be cured by rubbing against the walls of a local chapel (my guidebook cautioned

that "exactly which part of the body is to be rubbed is not clear"), and the sight of mermaids combing their hair on a certain footbridge — not an infrequent occurrence, apparently — is considered a sure sign of future business success.

The guidebooks are half right, at least. There is magic on the island, but it has nothing to do with curative chapels or well-coiffed mermaids. It's a magic that resides in silvery shingles on a mountain of cross-topped domes, in multi-towered silhouettes that rise like a mirage or a fever-dream, in the reassurance that it's all right to enjoy old buildings just because they're such a rich feast for the unhurried eye.

I've told friends that if I turn up missing, they can assume I've gone back to Kizhi. If they come looking for me, I'll be easy to spot: I'll be the one staring open-mouthed, muttering "Wow."

Cheeky Symbol of the New South

Travelers' Alert: If you drive north-ward over Red Mountain en route to downtown Birmingham, Ala., on 20th Street, you will be mooned.

The mooning is not exactly a close-up, in-your-face sort of confrontation, but it happens. Just as you reach the crest of the mountain, you'll see it clearly: a bare…(how shall I put this?)…*derriere* looming through the trees to your left. And I do mean "looming" because it's not just naked, it's enormous.

The posterior in question belongs to Vulcan, who's been providing a cheeky (sorry, I just couldn't resist) welcome to his hometown for more than half a century. This is the culmination of a career that began in St. Louis, where he was Alabama's exhibit at the 1904 World's Fair. Created by sculptor Giuseppe Moretti, the 57-foot-tall figure of the mythological god of metalworking was the largest iron statue in the world. When the fair closed, he came home to Birmingham.

Vulcan spent several years at the state fairground before the Works Progress Administration built him a proper home on Red Mountain, where he was hoisted onto a handsome 124-foot-tall stone pedestal. His elevated perch makes him clearly visible from all over the city — even at night because he holds an electric beacon that glows red

to indicate a local traffic fatality that day. (I sometimes think this is a demeaning job for a god, but then I also suppose that being the toast of a World's Fair makes being listed in the National Register — an honor bestowed on Vulcan in 1976 — seem like pretty small potatoes.)

Legends have grown up around him. A statue called "Electra" stands atop the Alabama Power Company Building downtown, and there are rumors that Vulcan meets her for an occasional clandestine midnight ren-dezvous. I give these stories no cre-dence. Sustaining the fires of passion would be difficult for these two: Vulcan wears only an apron and Electra wears even less, and Birmingham midnights can be chilly. Besides, how easy is it to be clandestine when you're of gargan-tuan size, made of metal and, in Electra's case, brightly gilded?

Vulcan has known his share of mishaps and indignities. Only a part of him (from the knees down) was in place for the opening of the 1904 fair. Back in Birmingham, he lay in pieces on a rail siding for two years while offi-cials debated his fate, and when he was re-erected, workmen attached his right hand and left arm incorrectly. At the fairground he was used to advertise a variety of products: For a while he even sported a pair of painted-on bluejeans. In a misguided "stabilization" effort in the 1930s he was filled with concrete up to shoulder level. A 1960s renovation transformed his pedestal into a slick modern shaft more appropriate for an astronaut than an ironworker.

He survived it all, but he's in trouble. He's badly cracked, probably because his iron skin and that concrete filling expand and contract at different rates. His anchorage and the framing of his left arm are unstable. Rust is a big problem. A Vulcan Task Force has recommended a complete restoration of the statue, the pedestal, and the park.

In a sense, concern over Vulcan's deteriorated state is part of a nationwide revival of interest in America's rich legacy of public sculpture. But it's more than that, because Vulcan is more than just a statue. He embodies the spirit and history of a whole city.

Birmingham lacks the hoopskirts-and-mint-juleps lineage that many Southern communities boast. The city was founded because deposits of limestone, coal, and iron ore made the site a natural center for industry. Lit by the hellish glare of furnaces where men sweated and swore, making iron and ushering in a new era, Birmingham was just the sort of place to make a blacksmith — even an Olympian one — feel right at home. Hard-muscled and proud, Vulcan is the perfect symbol of the place where the New South was born.

So here's a plea to the powers that be in Birmingham: Give Vulcan the respectful care he needs and deserves. Not every city has its own mountaintop deity. You're lucky to have this one, bare bottom and all.

UPDATE: Faced with mounting evidence that chunks of the Big Guy might start falling off at any time, the City of Birmingham made the laudable decision to undertake a complete restoration of Vulcan and his pedestal. In the fall of 1999, workers began disassembling the statue and reaming out the concrete that had been poured into its core. Current plans call for the statue to be reassembled and reinstalled — on a restored stone pedestal in a re-landscaped park — by mid-2003. Instead of a traffic-fatality beacon, the newly buffed-up blacksmith will hold a spear point in his hand, just as he did at the St. Louis Fair.

The restoration project hasn't been totally non-controversial. One local resident filed suit to halt Vulcan's return to his mountaintop perch, claiming that the statue is a religious symbol and therefore inappropriate for a public park. Most people, however, appear to be delighted that Birmingham's Iron Man has been given a new lease on life. I'm one of them.

HEADACHES

You know how it is when you own an old house: There's always something that needs fixing. Since the National Trust owns a slew of old houses and a whole mess of out-buildings, the work never ends. It's like painting the Golden Gate Bridge: By the time you get it done, it's time to start over again.

These days our collection of museum properties is a collection of construction sites, with workers busy at projects ranging from seismic retrofit to bowling-alley restoration, from finding a new use for a pony barn to dismantling and re-erecting an entire house. Not your typical weekend handyman's to-do list.

Take that "seismic retrofit" item, for instance. Many visitors to Filoli, the Trust's grand estate south of San Francisco, are unaware that the San Andreas Fault runs along the property's western edge. While the mansion escaped serious damage in the 1989 Loma Prieta earthquake, proper stewardship requires something more than merely trusting to continued good luck. To make the house as "quake-proof" as possible, tons of steel and concrete bracing have been installed over the past several months, most of it slipped into roomy cavities that the architect, for reasons that are unclear, left between the interior and exterior walls. The beefed-up mansion walls should be able to withstand a pretty good shaking.

The average homeowner is rarely called upon to restore a bowling alley, but the Trust owns two of them. The alley at Lyndhurst in New York's Hudson Valley (the other is at Montpelier, by the way) is the center-piece of a turn-of-the-century playhouse that also sported game rooms and breezy verandas overlooking a tennis court. During World War II owner Anna Gould threw the building open to servicemen, but in more recent years it was a near-ruin sealed off behind a chainlink fence. Not any more. When the restoration crew (which has included summer interns from several countries) finishes its work, the building will be open to visitors and will house many of Lyndhurst's educational programs for children. Soon there'll be laughter again where the Goulds and their guests once amused themselves in grand style.

On my first visit to Montpelier in Virginia, I fell in love with the pony barn, situated on the edge of a beautiful rolling field that my guide called the "yellin' pasture." (I pondered the meaning of this title — Was it the site of some boisterous primitive ceremonial, or just a place where troubled souls could holler their hearts out? — until I realized that the guide was actually saying "yearling pasture.") With its warm wooden walls and lofty spaces, the pony barn looked like a terrific place to live. I was ready to move in, but the Montpelier staff had other ideas. Thanks to a generous donor, the pony barn is undergoing a top-to-bottom renovation for use as an education center. Since most users of the new facility will be schoolchildren, the term "yellin' pasture" may turn out to be accurate after all.

Meanwhile, Frank Lloyd Wright's Pope-Leighey House is laying claim to the title of "America's Most Frequently Built House." In its original location the house stood in the path of a proposed highway, so in 1961 it was taken apart and reconstructed on the grounds of Woodlawn Plantation in Virginia. Unfortunately, the new site lay atop an underground vein of slippery clay, so over the past several years half of the house has exhibited a resolute determination to slide downhill. The resulting cracks in the concrete floor eventu-

ally got so big that there was spirited debate over whether they should properly be called chasms or merely crevasses. The only way to remedy the situation was to dismantle the house and rebuild it — again — on a clay-free site just a few yards away. While the process is fascinating (you don't often get a chance to see a Frank Lloyd Wright building under construction), we're hoping this move will be the last. The Pope-Leighey House wasn't meant to be a mobile home.

There's more: new visitors' centers at Lyndhurst and Filoli, chimney stabilization at Brucemore, a new research library at Drayton Hall, landscape restoration at Shadows-on-the-Teche. When it's all done, when the plaster dust settles and the discarded nails and leftover scraps of wood are cleared away, we're looking forward to taking a breather.

But not for long. You know how it is when you own an old house.

Past Forgetting

The folks at Colonial Williamsburg, in a laudable effort to inject a jolt of reality into their re-creation of 18th-century life, have begun staging reenactments of slave auctions and other gruesome vignettes of life under slavery. These events aren't always well received. Apparently, some visitors who have come to the restored area in search of gingerbread and tulips and tricorn hats don't want to be reminded that the Good Old Days had some decidedly bad aspects.

Whether we admit it or not, most of us like our history simple and slick, in bite-size doses and, if possible, sugar-coated so it'll go down easy. Fighting that preference for sunshine and happy endings is what the recently formed International Coalition of Historic Site Museums of Conscience is all about.

Every historic site has a story to tell, of course. What sets Coalition sites apart is the fact that the stories they tell are set in the dark, bloody corners of human experience. They deal unflinchingly with subjects such as economic oppression, racial and ethnic hatred, warfare, and genocide.

The roster of member sites reads like the table of contents in an encyclopedia of misery. There's the Maison des Esclaves in Goree, Senegal, for instance: a fortress-like structure where thousands of enslaved Africans were held before being shipped off to the plantations, mines, and workshops of the New World. The gloomy Workhouse in Nottinghamshire is a forbidding reminder of the consequences of poverty in 19th-century Britain, and New York's Lower East Side Tenement Museum (a National Trust Historic Site) preserves the harsh living conditions endured by immigrants who sought a better life in America. In the vast sweep of central Russia, the cluster of modest buildings known innocuously enough as Perm-36 is the best-preserved remnant of the extensive network of labor camps that made the very name "Siberia" a fearsome synonym for exile and imprisonment in the Stalinist era. The Liberation War Museum in the teeming city of Dhaka catalogs atrocities that occurred during Bangladesh's 1971 war of independence from Pakistan, while an initiative called "Memoria Abierta" in Buenos Aires memorializes those who suffered, died, or disappeared between 1976 and 1983 during Argentina's brutal military dictatorship.

At these sites, the power of place is inescapable: At the Maison des Esclaves, the simple doorway through which men and women in chains were herded onto ships speaks volumes about the terrible finality with which slaves' ties to their homeland were severed.

But the Coalition's mission goes beyond preserving buildings and artifacts. Sites are committed, in the words of the 1999 charter, to "stimulating dialogue on pressing social issues and promoting humanitarian and democratic values." Instead of isolating themselves behind velvet ropes, the sites form partnerships with social agencies, provide care and shelter for homeless children, hold land courts to settle property disputes, publish guides for new immigrants, train young people as "history ambassadors," and host conferences on human-rights abuses.

In short, they struggle, as all historic sites do, against the natural tendency to forget or sanitize the past. But they also work, as too many historic sites don't, to help people use the memory of past abuses as a foundation for a more humane and livable society.

I'm not going to repeat the adage that says those who don't remember history are condemned to repeat it — oops, sorry, it slipped out — but it's a simple fact that we humans have done some appalling things to one another in the past, and we demonstrate a disturbing willingness to keep doing them until someone stops us.

Maybe that's the best metaphor for these insistently unpleasant and absolutely essential places: They are stop signs on the slippery road leading back into the shame-haunted, gore-spattered abyss where we've already spent too much time. We need these places, even if we don't like what they tell us about ourselves. In fact, we need them precisely because the mirror image they present doesn't show our best side.

Want to be challenged, discomfited, maybe even changed? Go visit a historic site that isn't afraid to shake a finger in your face. Want a pretty sugar coating? Go buy some M&Ms.

UPDATE: The Coalition continues to grow — an indication of the vast and murky reservoir of misdeeds that mankind has to answer for. According to the Coalition's website (www.sites-ofconscience.org), several American sites have recently become members, among them the National Civil Rights Museum in Memphis, the Women's Rights National Historical Park in Seneca Falls, N.Y., and the Japanese American National Museum in Los Angeles.

Right Here

It's a classic movie moment: Drake McHugh, played by a youthful Ronald Reagan, wakes up in a hospital bed to find that his legs have been amputated. Staring wild-eyed at the place where his legs should be, he screams, "Where's the rest of me?" That melodramatic scene from *Kings Row* kept running through my mind on a recent trip to Texas.

My stepfather's parents lived in a tiny East Texas town called Keene, and I always looked forward to visiting them. Their house had screened porches front and back, with a big table where we ate in warm weather and a glider on which my sister and I swung faster and faster until some grownup yelled at us to stop. Best of all, I got to sleep in the attic, beside a window that looked out over my grandmother's iris beds and the fields that rolled off beyond the fence.

To a kid from the treeless, pancake-flat plains of West Texas, the countryside around Keene seemed foreign and exotic, so lush as to be practically Edenic. There were woods to wander in and little streams to throw rocks into. And there were hills to climb — minimalist hills that probably wouldn't even register on a topographical map, but they kept the horizon from being ankle-high and ruler-straight as it was back home.

Because it played an important role in my life for a good many years, I decided to pay a visit to Keene when I was in Texas recently. I hadn't been there in years, so I expected to find things changed. But when I pulled off the highway into the town, things got weird.

Keene was gone. More precisely, the Keene I remembered had been replaced with something I didn't recognize. I drove around for most of an hour, finding *nothing* that looked familiar. A street sign reading "Old Betsey Road" rang a bell, but the Old Betsey Road I remembered was an unpaved country lane, while this was a broad, roaring river of cars. After several uneasy minutes, I recognized the stone gateway at the entrance to the little Seventh-Day Adventist college in the middle of town. But the cluster of modern buildings beyond the gateway looked nothing like the college I remembered, and the street leading up to the campus — the street where the post office used to be — seemed to have vanished.

I wanted to find my grandparents' house, but I had no idea where to look for it. I suppose I could have asked for directions ("Do you remember some people named Young who used to live somewhere around here in a white house with a glider on the front porch and some irises out back and a bed in the attic?"), but I didn't. Maybe I was afraid they'd tell me the house had been torn down years ago. Besides, I was beginning to hear poor, legless Drake McHugh screaming from that hospital bed, and it was giving me the creeps. I drove back to the interstate and headed for someplace familiar.

So what does all this mean? I'm still trying to sort it out, but here's what I've concluded so far:

There are three good reasons for saving older buildings. First, they're good to look at, and we should save them because they give our communities grace-notes of beauty, variety, and visual texture. Second, they have an almost infinite capacity for reuse, and we should save them because it's good sense (and sound ecological practice) to do so. Third, they are tangible links with history, and we should save them as a means of maintaining connections with a past that we need to remember.

As I get older, this last reason seems increasingly important.

More than a century ago, John Ruskin said this about architecture: "We may live without her and worship without her, but we cannot remember without her." Remembering is essential, and the task of avoiding amnesia is much easier when we can see the past and touch it and live with it. There's something incredibly powerful about being able to walk into a building and say, "This is where it happened, within these walls, right *here*."

That's what a landmark does: It tells you, "Right here." Without landmarks to guide you, you get lost. Everybody knows that, but somehow I never grasped the real truth of it until I looked for part of me in Keene and couldn't find it.

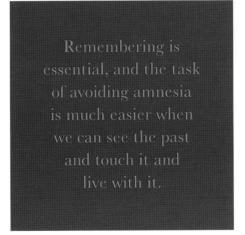

Remembering is essential, and the task of avoiding amnesia is much easier when we can see the past and touch it and live with it.

Sic Transit

Sometime during the summer, worn down by the pleas of friends and family, I will agree to spend the day at a theme park. Having forked over a small fortune to gain admittance, I will pass several hours strapped into contraptions that spin, shake, jolt, drench, and plummet. At frequent intervals I will pause in my revels to eat things that I ordinarily wouldn't touch with a ten-foot fork. When I finally crawl home, parts of me will be beet-red (sunburn), other parts of me will be pea-green (nausea), and all of me will be thoroughly exhausted.

It happens every year. And every year I become more convinced that our Victorian forebears had the right idea: When they wanted a pleasant excursion, they went to the cemetery.

It began with the opening of Mount Auburn Cemetery in Cambridge, Mass., in 1831. Before then, most burials took place in churchyards, many of which eventually found themselves surrounded by bustling commercial districts, increasingly crowded, and perceived as threats to public health. Mount Auburn was different. Modeled after Pere-Lachaise cemetery in Paris, it offered winding paths, deep-shaded groves, and grassy meadows, exemplifying the romantic appreciation for the beauties of nature popularized in the works of Emerson and Thoreau, Thomas Cole and A. J. Downing. At a time when few cities had public parks, it was an oasis, a place for strolling and having picnics — as well as being buried.

Mount Auburn's success led to the establishment of "rural cemeteries" all over the country: Laurel Hill in Philadelphia, Spring Grove in Cincinnati, Woodlawn and Green-Wood in New York, Graceland in Chicago, and scores of others. Today, just as their designers intended, these cemeteries are delightful places (yes, you can use "cemetery" and "delightful" in the same sentence) to spend a few hours.

They offer a display of sculpture matched by few museums. While there is a banal sameness to the heavy-lidded angels and sleeping children that adorn many graves, some monuments are quite compelling. A haunting, enigmatic bronze figure by Augustus Saint-Gaudens draws art connoisseurs from all over the world to Washington's Rock Creek Cemetery, and Philadelphia's Laurel Hill boasts a memorial by Alexander Calder that depicts a soul escaping from a coffin. (It turns out, in case you're wondering, that a soul resembles a hybrid comprising equal parts of cloud, flame, and amoeba.) Stone after stone displays the sculptural vocabulary of death and mourning

— urns, willows, floral wreaths, broken columns — often rendered with great skill. One of the most striking images I've seen was carved near the top of a tall obelisk: a disembodied hand pausing in its heavenward flight to drop the chains that had bound it to mortality.

Cemeteries also offer a crash course in architectural history. At Woodlawn in the Bronx, millionaire O. H. P. Belmont is buried in a miniature French Gothic cathedral, while F. W. Woolworth rests nearby in an Egyptian temple guarded by bosomy sphinxes. Surrounding them are tombs inspired by the Parthenon and the Pantheon, others displaying the influence of H. H. Richardson and Louis Sullivan, and even a few examples of Art Deco.

Sometimes there are surprises. Marking President James Monroe's grave at Hollywood Cemetery in Richmond, Va., is an elaborate cast-iron confection that looks like an enormous — and spectacular — Gothic birdcage. And every time I go to Oak Ridge Cemetery in Springfield, Ill., to pay my respects at the tomb of Abraham Lincoln, I find myself mesmerized by another mausoleum nearby. It's in the form of a Greek temple — columns, pediments, the whole classical works — but it's rendered in a primitive style so crude as to be downright troglodytic. If I didn't know better, I'd swear Fred Flintstone is buried there.

Among the thousands of epitaphs I've read over the years, two stand out as particular favorites. One is in Richmond, Va. The headstone bears a nicely detailed carving of an old-fashioned locomotive and a poem that describes a railroad man's journey to paradise:

His time card full, no wages docked,
His name on God's payroll,
And transportation through to Heaven,
A free pass for his soul.

My other favorite marks the resting place in Key West, Fla., of a hypochondriac waitress who apparently endured years of unacknowledged suffering. The inscription is brief and defiant, valediction and vindication: "*I told you I was sick.*"

GOING TO TOWN

Judging by their cries for help, some communities are having a hard time holding on to their historic library buildings. Happily, that isn't the case here in Washington, D.C. Our elegant old Carnegie Library, a monumental marble pile that has presided over Mount Vernon Square since 1902, is being turned into a museum.

I can hear you muttering under your breath — especially those of you who have trudged through the National Museum of Everything Ever Created by Man or Nature that occupies several jam-packed buildings on the Mall. "Just what Washington needs," you're saying, "another museum."

In fact, we really do need this one. Instead of exhibiting Nineteenth-Century Patchwork Quilts or Carnivores of the Serengeti, this new museum will celebrate the city we Washingtonians call home.

I recently took a hardhat tour of the museum-to-be. *[Note to self: Do not for a moment delude yourself that you look cool in a hardhat.]* Outside, the building's neoclassical columns and arches loomed serenely above the clutter of construction trailers and chain-link fences. Inside, the once-hushed library rooms echoed with the kind of semi-controlled pandemonium you'd expect at a worksite where Opening Day is bearing down like a runaway freight train.

Here's what I learned on my tour: One of the City Museum's most important features will be the exit.

A major goal of the institution is to entice visitors — residents and tourists alike — to go out and explore the real Washington, the one that doesn't often show up on postcards. This is a terrific idea. If it works, visitors will see something unexpected and wonderful. For starters, instead of besieging the hot-dog vendors near the Mall, they might head to the Shaw neighborhood, where the United House of Prayer dishes out some of the best soul food they'll ever taste, or the area called Adams Morgan, which has more Ethiopian restaurants than anyplace outside of Addis Ababa.

My city gets a bad rap from newscasters, office-seekers, and dissidents. They're always saying things like "Washington announced today…" or "Washington is robbing us blind" — making "Washington" a synonym for "faceless bureaucracy" or "boundless evil." Those of us who live here are more apt to call the place "D.C." — and it simply means "home." We say it with pride and occasional frustration, and with the smugness that comes from knowing the city's secrets.

We know, for instance, how dogwood and redbud turn the upscale enclaves of Chevy Chase and Cleveland Park into a riot of color every spring — but we know we can see equally dazzling hues on the Sunday-morning streets of Brookland and Petworth, where lavishly-hatted ladies cluster on church steps like bright birds. We know about 8th Street S.E., where a short stroll takes you from Eastern Market (home-grown produce and a flea market full of remarkable stuff you never knew you needed) to the historic Marine Barracks (parade-ground pageantry guaranteed to raise a goosebump) to nightspots where you can try line-dancing or stand around a piano and belt out show tunes. We know 16th Street N.W., which has one of everything — including Washington's last remaining H.H. Richardson building, a park that looks as if it belongs in Italy, and a Vietnamese church painted in Day-Glo colors. And one-block-long Ridge Street N.E., lined with tiny houses that look like the dens of a colony of urbanized hobbits. And Dupont Circle, where there's a coffee shop on every block, diplomatic limousines cruise past hand-holding same-sex couples, kamikaze bicycle messengers take a breather beside the fountain, and shirt-sleeved lawyers play chess with dread-locked street philosophers.

We all have our favorite home-town places. One of mine is residential Capitol Hill, where long streets of tidy rowhouses may end in a tree-framed close-up of the Capitol dome or a distant glimpse of the Basilica of the Immaculate Conception. I rarely see tourists on those streets, but maybe that's about to change. That would be a good thing.

The City Museum opens in May, just in time for vacation season. Consider this your invitation to visit the National Trust's hometown. Come see the national icons, by all means — but then stay to see the city beyond the monuments.

WHITELAW MEMORIES

According to the calendar, Black History Month is over. But at 13th and T Streets in Washington, D.C., the celebration continues in a building with WHITELAW carved in stone above the door.

Whitelaw. While it actually refers to the man who built the place, the name has symbolic overtones as well. It was white man's law that made the building necessary.

Washington in 1919 was a firmly segregated place. In November of that year, the Whitelaw opened as the first apartment hotel in the city — and one of the first in the country — built exclusively for black patrons. What *The Washington Bee* called a "mammoth monument to the Negro's thrift and energy" was the fulfillment of John Whitelaw Lewis's dream. Within the span of a few years Lewis had risen from apprentice mason to founder of one of the first black-owned banks in the United States. Eager to share his prosperity, he determined to build a facility that would provide (in the words of the recent application for landmark designation of the Whitelaw) "a dignified and gracious setting for the social expression of an excluded race."

Funds for erecting the Whitelaw were solicited from black citizens who bought stock in the project at $12 a share. The architect, Isiah T. Hatton, was a black man, and construction was carried out by an all-black crew. On a fundamental level the Whitelaw was the bricks-and-mortar emblem of local African-Americans' pride in themselves. They needed it: Four months before the hotel opened, nine men were killed in a Washington race riot.

The Whitelaw ballroom, which boasted stained-glass ceiling panels and elaborate plasterwork, was as pretty as any public room in the city. But from the very beginning, the important thing about the Whitelaw was not how it looked, but what it was. It was where everything happened. Everybody who was anybody slept there, partied there, or just went there to see and be seen. The hotel offered lodging to a "who's who" of celebrities — including performers in the theaters on nearby U Street, then in its heyday as America's "Great Black Way" — for whom most other local hotels were off-limits. The guest register was signed by everyone from Joe Louis to Duke Ellington, George Washington Carver to Redd Foxx.

Ironically, the end of segregation marked the end of the Whitelaw's glory days. Then riots in 1968 scarred the neighborhood. The hotel hung on for another decade, the shadowy turf of hookers and drug dealers, before finally closing its doors in 1977. Four years later, a fire destroyed much of the building's interior.

Then came a miracle — and a happy ending. A nonprofit housing developer called Manna, Inc., bought the Whitelaw in 1991. Assembling a complex financial package that included the federal rehab and low-income housing tax credits, Manna gutted the upper floors to provide 35 apartments for low- and moderate-income tenants. In recognition of its importance to the community, the ballroom was meticulously restored. The building was rededicated in November 1992.

On a cold Saturday recently, Manna held an Open House at the Whitelaw. I went, liked what I saw, and was about to leave when two women of a certain age walked into the gleaming ballroom and gazed around approvingly. They had been in this room before; for them, the place was crowded with faces and sounds that the rest of us could not see or hear. They smiled and pointed and smiled again. *Remember that party? I sat*

> But from the beginning, the important thing about the Whitelaw was not how it looked, but what it was.

right there, in that blue dress I loved so much. And the flowers and the music — remember?

The pair moved across the room to examine a display of photos and pages from old guest registers. Leaning in close, one of them reached up to tap the face in a faded advertisement. "Look at that," she said. "Cab Calloway. Did you ever go see him at the Howard Theater?"

"Sure did," her companion answered. "More than one time. Wasn't he something?"

"That man could really put on a show."

"MMMMMMmmmmmHMMMMM mmmmm."

These women slopped through a couple of inches of slush to get there that morning. Something told me they'd walk through a howling blizzard just to have dinner at the Whitelaw again and then go over to catch Cab Calloway's late show at the Howard.

They were still talking quietly to each other when I walked outside into bright sunshine. The wind was cold, but it felt like spring at 13th and T.

Unreal Victories

There's been another skirmish in the never-ending battle of Real vs. Slick, and it appears that Slick has won this round.

Lower Broadway in Nashville, Tenn., has always been a less-than-elegant thoroughfare, and in recent decades it has slid into an agreeable sort of scruffiness. It has some vacant storefronts, a pawnshop or two, an "adult" bookstore, and a sprinkling of bars where, on any given night, you can listen to a bunch of would-be country music stars trying out their torch-and-twang. There are harbingers of upscale renewal — rehabbed facades, a couple of new restaurants, a huge new sports arena — but much of Lower Broadway is still what it always was: a fairly ordinary, somewhat funky downtown street. In other words, it's Real.

For years the Metro Historical Commission has been working to preserve Lower Broadway's historic buildings and revitalize the area without glitzing it up too much. Keeping a place Real is a challenging task — as the commission learned on Second Avenue, a downtown street of handsome Victorian buildings that has been transformed in recent years into a lively enclave of shops, galleries, restaurants, and loft apartments. Some local preservationists think that Second Avenue is

perilously close to becoming Slick, and they're afraid that the same thing might happen on Broadway.

Their anxiety level rose considerably when Planet Hollywood arrived. First the movie-themed restaurant gave the old Alamo Building a jarring new paint job. Then came the sign — a big, gaudy revolving globe jutting over the Broadway sidewalk. The Metro Historical Commission opposed the sign, saying that it was overscaled and that it compromised the neighborhood's architectural and historical integrity. Others claimed the commission was just being obstinate and inflexible. They said the restaurant should be applauded for its willingness to invest in the revitalization of a shabby street. When all the shouting was done, the sign stayed. Planet Hollywood is doing a booming business.

So Slick has established a beachhead on Lower Broadway. That's not exactly disastrous, but it is ominous. Slick drives out Real every time. That's bad news for places like Tootsie's Orchid Lounge, located just a block — and a world — away from Planet Hollywood.

To call Tootsie's a dingy, smoky little bar is to slight its status as a Nashville institution. Back when the Grand Ole Opry was housed in the nearby Ryman Auditorium, Tootsie's was famous as the watering hole where stars dropped in for a beer between shows. But since the Opry moved to a new venue out on the edge of town — another victory for Slick, though the Ryman still hosts some performances — Tootsie's has survived mostly on its memories and the patronage of diehard fans who come in to experience the feel and smell of a place with 50 years' worth of hope, heartbreak, and cigarette smoke soaked into its walls.

Tootsie's is Real, a reminder of what Lower Broadway and the world of country music used to be.

> Tootsie's is Real, a reminder of what Lower Broadway and the world of country music used to be.

And if Lower Broadway goes the way of other downtown historic districts from coast to coast, trading its own unique character for big-name, big-bucks, assembly-line Slick, Real places like Tootsie's may be doomed.

Does successful revitalization inevitably lead to the proliferation of Victoria's Secrets and Hard Rock Cafes that makes one historic district look pretty much like another? I hope not, but the evidence seems to be against me.

Can Tootsie's and Planet Hollywood coexist on Lower Broadway? I hope so, but I'm skeptical.

Does it even make sense to worry about this, or is revitalization worth whatever it takes — even an avalanche of Slick that turns Real streets into theme-park parodies of themselves? I can't answer that one.

One more thing: Soon after Planet Hollywood opened, another Broadway merchant announced that he wanted to put up a big sign, too. Since he sells barbecue, he naturally wanted a sign with a pig on it — a happy-faced pink pig wearing a top hat, to be precise. "It'll be in good taste," he said. I'm still trying to decide whether that's a promise or a threat.

UPDATE: The question of whether Tootsie's and Planet Hollywood can coexist is now moot, since Planet Hollywood closed its restaurant on Lower Broadway in 2001. Tootsie's, meanwhile, is still going strong. Check out www.tootsies.net to see what's going on — or to join the World Famous Tootsies Orchid Lounge Fan Club.

LAMENT FOR A POLYNESIAN PARADISE LOST

WITH APOLOGIES TO OGDEN NASH

You're sure to beat your breast and cry "O me O my O"
When I tell you what has happened in Ohio.
I'm talking about the fair city of Columbus, to be specific,
Where the forces of destruction have severed a remarkable link
    between Midwest America and South Pacific.
Here's the story in a nutshell:
    The Polynesian supper club called the Kahiki
Is gone, and merely writing the words makes my eyes go all leaky.

Back in the 50s and 60s, when people spent a lot of time worrying about
    nuclear fallout and the Berlin Wall and other distressing topics,
Places like the Kahiki provided a welcome opportunity to slip off for an
    evening in the Tropics.
With their tiki torches and scowling idols and waitresses wearing sarongs
And background music by Martin Denny, who made a career out of
    soothing pseudo-South Seas songs,
These places could calm the most hard-core psychotic
Just by being so wackily, endearingly exotic.
The ceiling, natch,
Was thatch,
And as for the rest of it, why would
You mind that it was mostly made of styrofoam and plywood?
You may turn up your nose and say it sounds like the Temple of
    Kitsch Victorious,
But I'm here to tell you, friends, that it was glorious.
There were few things more pleasant for a gal and her fella
Than to lean back and sip something served in a coconut shell with a
    little paper umbrella.
Even in the midst of mid-Ohio dry land,
You could pretend you were marooned with Ginger on *Gilligan's Island*,
And the rest of the world hardly seemed to matter
After an hour or so spent dawdling over a Flaming Volcano and a
    PuuPuu Platter.

Destinations

I'd give you the Kahiki's address, but
　　if you went there, you'd look
　　around and ask, "Where's the durn
　　thing at?"
Because a couple of months ago they
　　smashed it flat.
Although it was nestled in the official
　　bosom of the National Register, the
　　owner decided it was smart
To sell the Kahiki as the site of a new
　　Mighty-Maxi-Mega-Mart.
The whole thing makes you wonder
Why in thunder
We should have to exchange a magical
　　place where the cocktails came in
　　primary colors and most of the
　　food was topped with a pineapple
　　slice and everything on the menu

had a name with at least two or three gleefully superfluous vowels
For another store full of underwear and snow blowers and paper towels.

But alas, the deed is done, and those moonlit Midwestern nights of muu-muus
　　and mai-tais are a thing of the past.
Aloha, Kahiki, I guess you were just too good to last.
Nowadays if you're in Columbus and you get a hankering for something
　　Polynesian, you have to go all the way to Tahiti.
Sorry, Sweetie.

Sagging Symbols

My uncle ran a grocery store in our home town. It was on 6th Street, but the actual address really didn't matter. When people asked where the store was, we just told them it was on the courthouse square. That was enough. Everybody knew where the courthouse was.

With its ungainly dome squatting atop walls of a singularly unattractive dirt-colored brick, it definitely was not a beautiful building. But its ugliness was irrelevant, like the looks of a beloved family member, because the courthouse was more than mere bricks and mortar.

In the midst of the vast, windswept West Texas landscape, the courthouse was the architectural paperweight that kept the town from blowing away. Built in 1910, just a few decades after the first settlements were established in our part of the state, it offered tangible evidence that our town was here to stay and that the residents were a civilized lot who knew what a public building ought to look like. More than that, it was a symbol — however clumsy — of the stability of democracy and the solemn grandeur of The Law.

Don't laugh. Converting abstract ideals and values into tangible reality was once considered a valid — even essential — function of architecture.

Our courthouse was the product of an age when buildings were designed to serve an important symbolic function, and architects worked hard to make them "fitting." Public buildings were intended to embody the awesome majesty of government itself and to make you feel both insignificant (a mere mortal in the presence of something mighty) and ennobled (a commoner doing business in a setting worthy of royalty).

A grand symbol demanded a grand setting, so many public buildings — especially courthouses — were sited in the middle of town, in a landscaped square where the town's most important monuments were installed. (On our own courthouse lawn, a windmill and a bandstand were joined every year by a big red thermometer that charted the progress of the annual Community Chest campaign.) Newspaper accounts described new public buildings with phrases like "highly artistic," "a noble specimen of fine architecture," and "a credit to the town." People took pride in them.

Whatever happened to that idea?

Today the notion that a public building should be edifying is as outmoded as a bustle. Here's how I know: I went to a post office the other day and couldn't find the front door.

It was in a medium-size southern city — but not downtown, where a post office should be. I parked in the vast asphalt lot, headed inside to buy some stamps — and stopped in my tracks. The facade of the building, probably built in the 1970s, was a featureless grid of glass and aluminum panels, any of which could have been a door. But which one?

On closer in-spection, two of the panels proved to have tiny metal plates inscribed "Push." I pushed, and found myself in a bare-walled, low-ceilinged space that had all the charm of a car-rental agency. I thought of my hometown post office, distinguished by a handsome stone arcade and a lofty lobby with brass grillwork and a WPA mural, and the real meaning of the tired phrase "they don't build them like that any more" came flooding in.

I'm starting to sound like Andy Rooney, so I'll close with a great court-house story:

Converting abstract ideals and values into tangible reality was once considered a valid — even essential — function of architecture.

When the old courthouse in Eastland, Tex., was torn down in 1926, officials were surprised to find a horned toad sealed inside the corner-stone. They were even more surprised when the animal, which presumably had been entombed for 30 years, revived. The miraculous lizard was named "Old Rip" and sent on tour — but not for long. Maybe three decades of stuffy solitude had left him ill-equipped to handle all that fresh air, or maybe it was the stress of show biz that did him in. Whatever the cause, six months after his resurrection Old Rip died. Today, the specially-commissioned casket that holds his embalmed remains is on dis-play at the courthouse.

Anyone in Eastland can tell you where to find it. Everybody knows where the courthouse is.

Doing Time

One day you stumble into a place that rings you like a bell, and you know that you'll keep winding up there, even if only in your mind, for the rest of your life. For me, that place is San Francisco. I first visited the city 30 years ago, lived there (much too briefly) 15 years ago, and have been back there on business or pleasure trips a dozen times since.

Most recently I went there for a week's vacation with my son, who was seeing San Francisco for the first time. In the course of some heavy-duty sightseeing — cable cars, Golden Gate Bridge, you know the drill — we signed up for something new: An Evening at Alcatraz.

It was, I'm happy to report, my first evening in a maximum-security prison. And it was not what I expected. It was much, much more.

The boat ride and the walk uphill from the dock were pleasant enough, but the experience really went into high gear with the audio tour of what everybody goes to Alcatraz to see: the cell house.

Settling the earphones on our heads, we walked through the door and into a nightmare. In yellowish half-light the cellblocks loomed above us, tiers of identical barred doors disappearing into the distance like a Piranesian exercise in perspective. After a few seconds, I was having trouble catching my breath and my heart was pounding. This is no exaggeration. There was something in the place, a vague miasma of cold, hard rage and despair and meanness that was as intriguing as it was unsettling. It felt like a really good horror movie: You're scared to death, and you want more.

The headsets carried the sounds of shuffling feet, of steel doors clanging shut. We wandered the shadowy corridors while the voices of former guards and inmates pointed out the sights and spun reminiscences. A guided tour of cold-walled hell: *This is D Block, where the worst cons were locked up. Step inside and see what it's like. That's the gun gallery, where the guards paced. When the wind was right, inmates in these cells could hear the sounds of parties at the yacht club, just a mile across the water.*

I had a great time that evening, and I wasn't the only one. My son suffered through many childhood hours in the back seat of our car while I took pictures of every old building in the worst parts of countless towns, so he might be forgiven for harboring a deep aversion to anything that smacks of history or preservation. But at Alcatraz, he was every bit as enthralled as I was. So was everyone else I saw, all of us rendered slack-jawed and speechless by the impact of the place, what we were hearing and feeling and learning.

Here's the point I want to make: That mind-expanding evening at Alcatraz, that creepy peek into an unfamiliar and unnerving world, was made possible by the National Park Service. That's right: The agency most of us associate with geysers and grizzlies is also in charge of The Rock.

In reviewing the current (and near-perennial) financial plight of the national park system, it helps to keep in mind that the Park Service operates under marching orders that might have been written by the Marx Brothers: "Okay, rangers, the place is all yours. Take care of these old buildings (watch out for that one in particular — it's really, really important, but it's about to fall down) and don't disturb the wildlife, even if it starts nesting on your desk. Keep the customers satisfied, which means listening to the most outrageous complaints and knowing the answer to every question imaginable — oh, and also keeping the restrooms clean. Here's a ridiculously small check that won't begin to cover your costs; stretch it as far as you can. And keep smiling." The amazing thing is, more often than not they manage to pull it off.

That evening at Alcatraz the Park Service showed me a side of history I'd never seen before — and gave me goosebumps in the process. When was the last time a federal agency did that for you?

UPLIFT

For reasons that are too personal to go into here, the past few months have constituted a massive pothole in the roadway of my life. To make matters worse, as if my own angst weren't enough, my hometown is currently chin-deep in a political mudwallow of backbiting, grandstanding, and generally trashy behavior. The combination of private turmoil and public tomfoolery has led me to spend a good many evenings staring into space — or worse, into the TV screen.

The other night I decided to go for a walk to clear my head. Acting on the premise that a high place is the best antidote to a low funk, I walked to the terrace on the west side of the Capitol — it's just a few blocks from my house — and stood at the balustrade looking down the length of the Mall, past the Washington Monument to the distant Lincoln Memorial.

(A parenthetical note: The Washington Monument looks weird these days. Encased in a cage of scaffolding for a top-to-bottom restoration, it's *fatter* than usual. The scaffolding gives off glints of metallic light, and its lacy grid makes the edges of the monument look soft and out of focus. It's a bit disconcerting, like seeing your mother in a punk hairdo, but sort of wonderful, too.)

The Mall at night is one of America's most awe-inspiring sights — the few tourists around me spoke in the hushed tones usually reserved for churches and banks — but on this particular night it didn't work for me. After several moments of trying to get lost in the view, I was still stubbornly dog-paddling through a swamp of gloomy thoughts. Then I turned around to face the looming bulk of the Capitol, and almost immediately my spirits began to lift.

It's the dome that does it. This architectural wedding cake celebrating the union of the states may be the best mood-elevator available without a prescription. I don't know how it works, or why. All I know is that looking at it takes me out of myself to a better place.

Abraham Lincoln understood that. The dome was half-finished when the Civil War erupted. There were some who thought that construction funds would be better spent on bullets and bayonets, but Lincoln wanted the dome completed as a symbol of the permanence of the Union and, by implication, of confidence in better days to come. The president prevailed, the work went on. Today, enshrined at the other end of the Mall, Lincoln must take enormous satisfaction in the symbol that he insisted be realized.

Lincoln (and architect Thomas U. Walter) gave us the best dome in the world. Better than Hagia Sophia in Istanbul, which gives you a sense of enclosed space that is almost mystically vast but looks sort of dumpy from the outside. Better than the Duomo in Florence, which is handsome and innovative, sure, but after 500 years still isn't finished, for pete's sake. Ours is an unequivocal gangbuster of a dome.

It's most impressive at night. Floodlit, it's snow-white, sugar-white, the whitest white you've ever seen, and against the dark sky it looks like a paper cutout pinned to a black velvet drape. With the windows in the drum glowing with light, it's downright airy — or at least as airy as anything with that much iron in it can be. You get the feeling that the statue of Freedom on top stands there primarily to keep the whole thing from floating away like a soap bubble.

Here's what it makes you think: If this beautiful thing exists — so grand, so right — and if it's been able to survive all that has happened under and around it, then maybe the world isn't going to hell in a handbasket after all, and maybe everything will be all right.

Lincoln wanted the dome completed as a symbol...

It was nearly 11:00 o'clock, with the wind getting colder and my neck stiff from craning upward, when I started for home. Just before turning the corner I looked back one last time. The dome gleamed, white as Everest and almost as tall.

Later I checked the dictionary to see whether "dome" is defined as "a lofty, white, noble thing that makes you feel better." It isn't, but it should be. I'm pretty sure Mr. Lincoln would agree.

UPDATE: Two things mentioned in this piece have disappeared from the Washington scene.

One, of course, is the scaffolding that encased the Washington Monument for several months. Designed by famed architect Michael Graves, it was almost universally hailed as an instant icon and a work of art in its own right — surely the first construction scaffolding to achieve that exalted status. Some of us were sorry to see it dismantled.

The other thing missing is the view from the west terrace of the Capitol. In the wake of the 9/11/01 terrorist attacks, the terrace was closed to visitors, and there's no word on when (or whether) it will be reopened. As a former frequent visitor to the site, I feel as if I've been separated from a dear friend.

PROLOGUES

The logs for Sukeek's cabin came from the forests of southern Maryland. The stones for the foundation came from the bank above St. Leonard Creek. Sukeek herself came from Africa. She was a slave.

The cabin was destroyed long ago by fire or weather or the simple passage of time. But archeologists and researchers, with enthusiastic help from some of Sukeek's own descendants, have been exploring the cabin site, trying to learn more about Sukeek and the world in which she lived. The site is in Calvert County, Md., at a place called Jefferson Patterson Park & Museum. It's a pretty cumbersome name, so lots of people just call it "Jeff Patt."

Calvert County is growing faster than just about anyplace else in Maryland. But once you get away from the new subdivisions and strip malls that have given Highway 4 a virulent case of road rash, it's still possible to find pockets of great tranquility here. Jeff Patt is one of those pockets. Looking over this sun-washed 550-acre swath of woods and fields sloping down to the Patuxent River, you might think it's a rural backwater where nothing ever happens. You'd be wrong. Things have been happening here for a very long time.

You can hardly stick a shovel into the dirt at Jeff Patt without turning up evidence of extensive Native American occupation, some of it dating back thousands of years. Early European colonists made their homes here, too. One of them was Richard Smith, the first attorney general of Maryland, who built a house (plus storehouses, barns, and slave quarters) close to the riverbank early in the 1700s. A century later, during the War of 1812, the largest naval battle in Maryland history took place here when British vessels traded fire with the war barges of the Americans' grandly named Chesapeake Flotilla. The remains of some of the barges are still buried in the silt a short distance offshore.

Scattered over the landscape are links with Jeff Patt's more recent history. The property's years as a model farm are reflected in a collection of buildings designed by Gertrude Sawyer, one of the handful of women to gain admission to the Old Boys' Club that was the American architectural profession in the early 20th century. In a new building that houses the Academy of Natural Sciences' Estuarine Research Center, scientists are investigating the impact of human activity on marine ecosystems. And in an even newer building nearby, the staff of the Maryland Archaeological Conservation Laboratory — arguably the best facility of its kind in the country — are conserving, studying, and curating more than 4.5 million artifacts from all over the state.

I read somewhere that the Cheyenne believe that everything that has ever happened in a place is still happening there. If that's true, Jeff Patt is a very crowded bit of geography. Hiking across a field, you pass a hastily constructed battery where young men sweat in their itchy uniforms and watch for British gunboats.

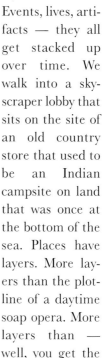

Idly throwing pebbles into the Patuxent, you pause to watch a couple of Indians pull oysters from the water and toss them into their canoe. Stooping to pick a wildflower, you rub elbows with slaves tending their owner's tobacco fields. Punching the keypad of your cell phone, you tap into a new world of instantaneous communication — while just over the hill, recently arrived English settlers are exploring a New World of a totally different kind.

History isn't linear, it's stratified. Events, lives, artifacts — they all get stacked up over time. We walk into a skyscraper lobby that sits on the site of an old country store that used to be an Indian campsite on land that was once at the bottom of the sea. Places have layers. More layers than the plotline of a daytime soap opera. More layers than — well, you get the idea. Keeping those layers intact (which, after all, is what preservation is all about) helps us realize what a tall stack of shoulders we stand on. That realization can be a bit unnerving — or enormously comforting. On a picnic at Jeff Patt as summer slides into fall, I choose the latter.

WE'VE GOT A LITTLE LIST

I'm crazy about lists. Asia's Tallest Mountains or History's Bloodiest Battles, Ten Worst Movies of the Year or Fifty Ways to Leave Your Lover — if it's a list, I'll read it.

I'm especially crazy about the World Heritage List. Maintained by the United Nations Educational, Scientific and Cultural Organization (UNESCO), this compilation aims to be the ultimate global honor roll of cultural and natural sites of "outstanding universal value." For a hardcore building watcher and armchair traveler like me, this is the A-list that trumps all other A-lists.

Initiated in 1972, the roster now comprises more than 700 sites from Afghanistan to Zimbabwe, from geological wonders such as the Grand Canyon to 20th-century creations such as Brasilia. Many are familiar icons — Yosemite, Chartres Cathedral, Machu Picchu — but others are probably unknown to most Americans. Hands up if you've ever visited Madagascar's Royal Hill of Ambohimanga or the Gochang, Hwasun, and Ganghwa Dolmen sites in South Korea. Been there, seen that? I thought not.

The 170-plus nations that have signed the World Heritage Convention are pledged to assist one another in preserving listed landmarks. According to a recent *National Geographic* article, the program has helped head off inappropriate development at the Pyramids and Victoria Falls, for example, and dues from member nations have provided funds to restore buildings, hire staff, and construct visitor facilities at several sites.

Scanning the list, I find myself fantasizing a trip that would encompass the historic towns of Diamantina in Brazil and Trogir in Croatia, the rock-hewn churches of Lalibela in Ethiopia and the gilded temples of Luang Prabang in Laos. I can't resist the lure of the Bwindi Impenetrable National Park in Uganda or, a bit closer to home, the Head-Smashed-In Buffalo Jump in Canada.

But then I notice something a bit unsettling: The U.S. isn't well represented on the list. The chateaux of France's Loire Valley are here, but the "cottages" of Newport aren't. The wooden churches of Maramures (Romania) are included, but not the adobe churches of the American Southwest. The historic centers of Havana and Santo Domingo are listed, but what about Savannah? Or New Orleans' French Quarter? Nope, nope, and nope. And don't even ask about more modern-day marvels such as Frank Lloyd Wright's Fallingwater or the Gateway Arch in St. Louis.

Of the 560-odd cultural treasures on the list, only *eight* are in the United

States. Italy, by comparison, has more than 30. Mexico has 20. The U.S. ranks just ahead of Bulgaria and Tunisia.

Blame bureaucracy. The nomination process in this country is cumbersome, to say the least. Before it can even be considered for nomination, a site must be designated a National Historic Landmark. That takes time. Then it must be placed on a so-called "Tentative List" and published in the *Federal Register* with adequate time for public comment. More delay. Finally, 100 percent owner consent to the nomination is required, a hurdle that is practically insurmountable in a historic district with hundreds of properties.

Blame fuzzy thinking too. Some members of Congress oppose placing any American sites on the list, holding that doing so would amount to surrendering our sovereignty to the United Nations. That's baloney, of course, but some people just can't rid themselves of the fear that swarms of UN helicopters will descend on us, delivering platoons of blue-helmeted furriners who will do unspeakable things to Thomas Edison's laboratory or the Empire State Building.

No U.S. site has been added to the list since 1995, and congressional opposition and public apathy make it highly unlikely that we'll see new nominations anytime soon. The U.S. Committee of the International Council on Monuments and Sites (US/ICOMOS), which facilitates American participation in international cultural conventions, has proposed sensible ways to make the nomination process a bit less byzantine, but nothing's happened yet.

So for now, we're allowing the World Heritage List to send out an embarrassing message: In the whole sea-to-shining-sea expanse of the United States, there are only eight cultural treasures of global significance. That's just plain wrong. I know it, you know it, and we ought to let the rest of the world know it too.

UPDATE: Several people were upset by this piece, and they wrote or telephoned to tell me so. One, for example, hoped that my opinions don't reflect the "official line" of the National Trust (they don't). Another scolded me for being part of a vast, malevolent "One World" conspiracy (I'm not) and yet another assured me that the UN has "practically taken over" much of the Alaskan wilderness (it hasn't).

The entire World Heritage List appears on the UNESCO website: whc.unesco.org/heritage.htm. It's possibly the best daydream-inducer available on the open market. New sites are sure to be placed on the list after the World Heritage Committee meets later this year, but don't look for any additions in the United States.

LIKE AN OLD SHOE

First it was *1984*. George Orwell's novel envisioned a future in which warfare was constant, Big Brother knew what was best for you, and daily life was bleak and pinched and sterile.

Then it was *2001*. Stanley Kubrick's movie showed us a future in which space stations twirled to a Strauss waltz, an ominous black slab floated around, and it was hard to figure out what it all meant.

Now it's almost 2003 — and the prognostications haven't amounted to much. We were warned that mankind would be enslaved by evil aliens from Alpha Centauri, but it hasn't happened. We were assured that someday our meals would be compressed into pills and we'd never again need dental floss, but that didn't happen either. We were promised bubble-topped cars that would drive themselves while we filed our nails or played Yahtzee, but they never showed up.

Let's face it, the future isn't what it used to be — and neither is our idea of how the city of the future should look.

At the 1939 New York World's Fair, visitors by the thousands lined up to get a glimpse of the "city of tomorrow" — a huge model of a metropolis in which everything was slick and shiny. A cluster of soaring towers downtown was ringed by suburbs where every flat-roofed, glass-walled house had a heliport in the backyard.

But in this impressive vision of a brave new world, old buildings and neighborhoods didn't exist. The place had no roots, no links with the shared history and traditions that give people and nations their identity. The trouble with this city of the future was that it had no past. It had no funky places. It had no Jimmy T's.

Jimmy T's is a small cafe on Capitol Hill in Washington, D.C. Here's what happens when you walk in on a Sunday morning: Cynde, working away at the grill, yells "Hi" and asks how you're doing and where you've been. From his station at the waffle iron, Cynde's husband John grins and nods. After you sit down, Bryan or Rick comes by to take your order and offer an irreverent (and generally dead-on) appraisal of your new hairstyle, tattoo, grandchild's photo, and/or breakfast companion. And then you settle in among the mismatched chairs and mismatched coffee mugs and consume a hearty helping of neighborhood life, seasoned with banter and gossip and cholesterol.

In his book *The Great Good Place* (Marlowe & Co., 1999), Ray Oldenburg laments the disappearance of community gathering places where people can linger, blow off steam, form and cement acquaintances. When critics accuse him of trying to bring back the past, Oldenburg replies, "We don't need the past. We need the places!"

He's mostly right, though I have to disagree with that "we don't need the past" bit. Jimmy T's wouldn't be the same if it were located in a new building in a strip mall instead of a rather shabby rowhouse, if its booths were un-scuffed and its tin ceiling freshly painted and its air perfumed with potpourri. What makes it special, what makes it so homey that you're

tempted to show up bathrobed and barefooted — what makes it, in short, the kind of place that we ought to fight hard to save if we're serious about creating and preserving real livability — is the years of use that have *earned* Jimmy T's its role as forum for, and ornament to, community life.

The kinds of places people really care about are rarely created from scratch. They evolve, they ripen and mellow. The city of the future isn't waiting to be built: It's here already, in the streets and neighborhoods where we live and work. We don't have to create it, we just have to ensure that it makes the transition from *today* to *tomorrow* without losing the ineffable, rooted character it has gained over time.

One memorable Sunday at Jimmy T's, the guy sitting at the counter beside me worked up the nerve to ask another customer for a date, and when she said yes, several of us applauded. If the city of the future doesn't have room for a place like that, I'm not sure I want to live there.

The National Trust for Historic Preservation is a private, nonprofit member-ship organization dedicated to protecting the irreplaceable. Recipient of the National Humanities Medal, the Trust provides leadership, education and advocacy to save America's diverse historic places and revitalize communities. Its Washington, D.C., headquarters staff, six regional offices and 21 historic sites work with the Trust's quarter-million members and thousands of local community groups in all 50 states.

For a subscription to *Preservation* magazine and to find out more about becoming a member of the National Trust, please call 1-800-315-NTHP. Use the promotion code APPA03 when you call and get $5 off your first year's dues!

National Trust for Historic Preservation
1785 Massachusetts Avenue, N.W.
Washington, DC 20036
www.nationaltrust.org

ISBN Number 0-89133-450-5

Project Manager: Elizabeth Byrd Wood
Printer: Mid-Atlantic Printers, Vienna, Va.
Designer: Chadick and Kimball, Washington, D.C.

ABOUT THE AUTHOR

Dwight Young has worked at the National Trust for Historic Preservation since 1977. He directed the National Trust's Southern Regional Office in Charleston, S.C., for seven years before coming to the Trust's national headquarters in 1984. He is the author of *Saving America's Treasures*, and his "Back Page" column appears in the Trust's bimonthly magazine, *Preservation*.

ILLUSTRATION CREDITS

Donald Christ: 67. Donna Reed Foundation: 68. Brett Emanuel: 5, 9, 17, 21, 27, 35, 39, 61, 77, 83, 97, 103, 111, 115. Heart of Danville, Inc., Danville, Ky.: 15. Steve Hall-Hedrich Blessing: 11. Mary Lou Gulley: 63. Ben Katchor, reprinted with the permission of The Wylie Agency, Inc. Copyright 1966: 53. Montpelier Foundation, James Madison's Montpelier: 89. National Trust for Historic Preservation: 41, 51, 79. National Park Service: 71. Rome Downtown Development Authority, Rome, Ga.: 47. San Francisco Convention & Visitors Bureau Photo: 107. Lynette Strangstad: 95. Mary Ann Sullivan: 57. Patrick Wood: 37. Dwight Young: 85. Tina H. Zeller: 23.